In a Caliph's Kitchen

This is for
LAITH
and
REEM
My two favorite pessoptimists

In a
Caliph's Kitchen

David Waines

RIAD EL-RAYYES
BOOKS

رياض الريس للكتب والنشر

56 Knightsbridge London SW1X 7NJ

In a Caliph's Kitchen

by
DAVID WAINES

First Published in Great Britain in 1989
Copyright © Riad El-Rayyes Books Ltd
56 Knightsbridge, London SW1X 7NJ

British Library Cataloguing in Publication Data

Waines, David
In a Caliph's kitchen
1. Food: Arab dishes – Recipes
I. Title
641.59′2′927

ISBN 1–869844–60–2

Designed by Alan Hamp
Photography by Anthony Dawton
Cooking and styling by Ian Fraser
Typeset by MS Filmsetting Limited,
Frome, Somerset, England
Printed by Milano Stampa
12060 Farigliano (CN) Italy

Contents

Baghdad and the new cuisine

The recipes gathered together in this volume have been selected from medieval Arabic culinary collections dating from the early ninth to the late thirteenth century (the third to the seventh century of the Hijra).[1] With two or three exceptions they are all, for reasons which will become apparent, from Iraq – the heartland of the domains of the Abbasid Caliphs (AH132–656/750–1258AD)*. The exceptions have been taken from works of Egyptian and North African provenance.[2] The selection is, however, representative of the great treasury of dishes which comprised the medieval urban culinary tradition. Apart from this, there is another aspect of historical interest in the collection; a number of the dishes reflect the genius of the ninth century author/compiler of the first practical and comprehensive cookbook in the Arabic language. And herein lies a story to be told.

Muslim writers of the medieval world called Iraq, 'the navel of the universe.' The epithet was appropriate and well deserved. For nearly half a millennium Iraq was the home province of the Abbasid dynasty, although for the major part of that time the ruling Caliphs were unable to exercise the full powers accorded them in the treatises of political theorists. Notwithstanding the weakness of the Caliphate, Iraq remained the fulcrum of the political life of the empire, and the land itself – the rich and fertile alluvial soil of the Tigris and Euphrates valleys – was a major source of the imperial treasury's wealth. It was this wealth that supported the cosmopolitan character of the imperial capital, Baghdad, and sustained it as the cultural emporium of the empire long after the political fortunes of the Caliphs had faded. Baghdad was, in the words of a contemporary, 'the market to which the wares of the sciences and the arts were brought, where wisdom was sought as a man seeks after his stray camels, and whose judgement of values was accepted by the whole world.'[3] The purveyors of cultural wares included the theologians, Koran reciters and commentators, experts on the Prophetic tradition and jurisprudents, poets and belletrists, philosophers, physicians and pharmacologists and the like, drawn from every corner of the far flung Abbasid domains, each contributing to the emergent, dynamic civilizational bloc that was Islamic.

The manifold literary expressions of Islamic culture form an intricate, complex mosaic; the major patterns are clearly discernible, yet certain minor motifs, albeit

* Where two dates are given, separated by a vertical stroke, the first is the Islamic reckoning, *anno Hegirae*, the second the Christian, *anno Domini*.

significant in themselves, have become effaced and so unable to display the full richness of their actual design. One such motif is the material life of medieval society, the manner and means by which people conducted the routine of their daily lives, feeding, clothing and housing themselves. That enduring reality, so immensely important, but which made so little noise.

One aspect within this broad spectrum of material life is the preparation of food. High medieval cultures display an almost uniformly consistent reticence about revealing the secrets (if such they were regarded) of their culinary traditions. Food has always been prepared in households, rich and poor, for their own members' consumption and the technology of early medieval cooking is known through the survival of kitchen artifacts. But how dishes were prepared, their particular ingredients, regional and class variations in diet are shrouded from modern scrutiny by the traditionally oral transmission of cooking lore over the centuries. In the European culinary tradition, for example, nothing seems to have survived by way of a practical cookery book between the fourth/fifth century compilation attributed to Apicius and an early fourteenth century fragment called simply *A Book of Cookery*. In China, the emergence of 'the world's first cuisine' according to one scholar can only be dated to the period of the southern Sung (AD1125–1279); the sources, however, appear to provide little guidance as to the preparation of specific dishes.[4] It is, therefore, something of a surprise – and a fortunate occurrence as well – that the culinary treasury of the entire medieval world is so richly endowed with literary remains in Arabic, its single most important source of recipes.

The story begins in Baghdad around the turn of the ninth century. The Abbasid domains flourished under the rule of the Caliph Harun al-Rashid (AH170–194/786–809AD), grandson of the Caliph al-Mansur who had founded Baghdad some forty years earlier. From an ancient site of pre-Islamic origin, Abbasid Baghdad burgeoned into the leading metropolis in the Islamic world. From the original circular, walled Caliphal complex called *Medinat al-Salam* (City of Peace) constructed on the west bank of the River Tigris, rapid growth by Harun's day had caused these early edifices to be engulfed by numerous bustling quarters. The capital, joined together by pontoon bridges, now sprawled along its eastern banks as well. The city was dotted with mosques and markets, the symbols of religious culture and commerce which alike contributed to its sparkling yet sober vitality. This was also the 'paradise on earth' of writers who celebrated Baghdad's wonderful gardens and orchards, its lush countryside, and not least, its magnificent high palaces with their sumptuously decorated gates and halls. The metropolis' population is impossible to estimate. A traditional calculation, based upon the number of unofficially recorded public baths, suggests that at its peak Baghdad had reached a figure of between a half and one million souls;[5] in any event, its probable size made it the largest contemporary urban conglomeration outside China.

It was in this milieu that a culinary *nouvelle vague* emerged. Among its many descriptive terms Baghdad earned renown too as the gastronomic 'navel of the universe'. It is our good fortune that the earliest extant Arabic work on the cooking arts provides so much information as to the creative forces behind this culinary movement. And, paradoxical as it may seem, while emerging within this urban milieu, Abbasid cuisine was essentially neither Baghdadi nor even urban in origin.

The emergence of the new cuisine should be set against the background of socio-economic developments of the early Abbasid period. One, of course, was the founding of the metropolis itself. Imperial cities like Baghdad (and such as Hangchow and Kaifeng in China) are political, economic and cultural centres of attraction which, like magnets, draw to them persons from widely scattered parts of the empire. These individuals bring with them their own local or regional cooking traditions; informally at first these traditions are placed in a common and increasing pool of culinary knowledge from which others can share. A wealthy and powerful court also plays an important, catalytic role in establishing the new cuisine: first, by setting standards of fashion eagerly imitated by the leisure class of courtiers, officers, bureaucrats, scholars, merchants and craftsmen; second, by dominating a rich and stable agricultural hinterland and by stimulating even more extensive commercial networks to distant regions. Thus the organizing power of the Caliphal government's bureaucracy became a yardstick of Baghdad's capacity to satisfy the gastronomic demands of the leisure elite with a ready supply of every imaginable food commodity. This prosperous class revelled in good food for its own sake; unhindered by taboos, or local likes and dislikes, but rather encouraged to 'eat of the good things God has granted.'[6] Once the original elements of the cuisine, the collective oral regional cooking traditions, were captured in written form, the recipe collections fixed a new tradition which then became subject itself to further experimentation and elaboration. It is in this second, more formal, stage that rural village and town fare would appear greatly transformed on the merchant's table as the new urban cuisine grew towards maturity. Unlike other aspects of the communal fund of folklore, such as poetry and popular tales, the detailed knowledge of cooking was confined largely to the domestic domain. But in the new urban context such as Baghdad that cooking lore had become public and, in time, part of a common national heritage.

However, underlying this process which was but a reflection of the rapid growth of Baghdad, there were concomitant explosions in the spheres of agriculture and commerce. Baghdad was the model, *par excellence*, of a medieval agro-city, an urban giant together with its rural hinterland from which it drew its basic food staples. Baghdad's rural hinterland, the Sawad and the Diyala plain, throughout the ninth century was the single most important source of grain and revenue in the empire. Although Iraq's fertile soil had sustained earlier dynasties and cultures, Abbasid Iraq was blessed in addition by what one scholar has called a 'medieval green revolution'.[7] This involved the introduction and diffusion of a number of food and fibre crops, notably from India, into the eastern Islamic world and thence westwards ultimately as far as Muslim Spain. Iraq was the gateway of this diffusion to the west. Some of the food items identified in this process are found in the recipes dating from the rise of the new cuisine in Baghdad. They include the aubergine and spinach. The green revolution may also have altered certain farming practices in the valleys of the Twin Rivers allowing for a new agricultural season in the summer; this permitted the productive use of previously idle land and labour. The increasing capacity of the countryside to export a growing surplus of food stuffs supported the expansion of urban areas like Baghdad.

Complementing Baghdad's agricultural hinterland was an even more extensive commercial network linking the capital by long distant trade routes to urban centres throughout the Abbasid empire and beyond. The development of new legal instruments, such as trade partnerships, facilitated the conduct of trade and the flexibility of these new institutions made Baghdad and its southern port of Basra a hub of international trading activity. As a consequence, Baghdad's food markets (apart from being provisioned with fruits and vegetables from local gardens and orchards) resembled a gourmand's gazetteer of the empire. From Syria came apples, pomegranates, plums, figs and apricots as well as fine olive oil; an oil made from violets and roses came from Kufa; saffron came from the Yemen and Isfahan, honey from Mosul, the best of which it was said should act like a blob of mercury when dropped on the ground; Tabaristan provided citrus fruits, Herat yielded currants; cane sugar came from Ahwaz, salted fish and buttermilk from Khwarizm, cloves, spikenard and nutmeg from India; quinces from Nishapur, figs from Hulwan and pears from Nihawand.[8]

The Caliphs, too, were able to command for their own use shipments of various regional specialities. In this manner some 30,000 containers of apples were ordered annually from Syria; 50,000 pounds of first grade sugar from Ahwaz; then 30,000 flasks of rosewater, 20,000 pounds of black raisins, 15,000 pounds of mango preserve, and 1,000 pounds of a honey and rosewater mixture called *julanjabin*, all from the province of Fars in Persia; 2,000 pounds of honey from Isfahan; 100,000 pomegranates and 1,000 pounds of dried peaches from Rayy (modern Tehran); and finally, from Khwarizm, a kind of melon called *baranj* was shipped to Baghdad in snow packed lead containers.

Between them, the court and the leisure class in Baghdad produced a sizeable corps of adventurous eaters who sought and found pleasure in the consumption of refined and subtle preparations. If courtly customs at table were to a degree ritualized, other segments of the urban populace experienced no such formal constraints. The new culinary culture was not confined to court circles alone yet neither was it accessible to the lower classes. As an anonymous poet bluntly observed, Baghdad was indeed 'a refreshment of souls for all mankind', but it was also a 'place of sorrow for the penniless'. The diet of the urban poor centered around the coarser and cheaper cereal grains, pulses, fish, dates, milk and its products, and occasionally the less well regarded kind of meat like beef. The worker's loaf was not the merchant's. And so, the appearance of a preparation in a cookbook, however humble its origin, meant that the culinary arts had transmuted it to delight a gourmet's palate. Baghdad's generation of 'new wave' gastronomes set the standards which others later followed.

The 'new wave' generation

The earliest known culinary works in Arabic appeared during the first half of the AH 3/9 AD century. None is extant complete. Fewer than one hundred recipes directly attributed to these first authors or compilers have survived in a late AH4/10AD century work.[9] The cookery books were but a small part of a broad, dynamic humanist literary movement which marked this period as a golden age of Arabic letters. The concern for food and drink in general, the art of cooking, the constitution of a proper diet and table etiquette were all treated as vital to a cultured person's preparation for life. The names are now known of nearly a dozen individuals who contributed to the literary expression of the culinary 'new wave'. They include Caliphs such as al-Ma'mun (d. 218/833) and al-Wathiq (d. 233–847) and al-Mu'tasim (d. 228/842), the poet Ibrahim b. 'Abbas al-Suli (d. 243/857), the physician Yuhanna b. Masawayh (d. 243/857), the courtier Yahya b. Khalid al-Barmaki (d. 190/805), the astrologer Yahya ibn abi Mansur al-Mawsili (d. not known), and one Abu Samin who remains unidentified but was perhaps a professional chef in the service of al-Wathiq. There are also recipes attributed to other individuals which were probably particular favourites of the persons concerned, or else dishes named especially in their honour. For example, dishes entitled *Haruniya* were so-called in honour of the Caliph Harun al-Rashid.

One figure, however, stands out from all these as the probable inspirational source for the others and undoubtedly the author/compiler of the first practical and comprehensive cookbook in the Arabic language. He was the younger half-brother of the Caliph Harun, the uncle of the Caliphs al-Ma'mun and al-Wathiq, friend of the physician ibn Masawayh and at least the acquaintance of the rest. His name was Abu Ishaq Ibrahim ibn al-Mahdi.

Ibrahim was born during the summer of 163/779 in the palace of al-Rusafa on Baghdad's east side.[10] All we know for certain of his early years is that his father, the Caliph al-Mahdi, died in a hunting accident when the prince was only six years old. Al-Mahdi is remembered as a just, cultured and generous ruler. He had a refined taste for the fare of the court kitchens yet was modest enough to enjoy a meal with a peasant or nomad while out hunting in the countryside. The young prince, Ibrahim, received the customary education from court tutors under the watchful eye of his mother Shikla, the beautiful and gifted concubine of al-Mahdi, and after his father's death under the supervision of Harun who became Caliph in 170/786.

Harun's court set new heights for extravagance and cultural brilliance where poets and singers were among the many who earned substantial rewards for their talents. Women, too, played no small role in the court's political and cultural life. Harun's mother Khaizuran and his wife Zubayba wielded considerable influence derived from their wealth and direct access to the Caliph. Moreover, highly trained singing girls were a regular feature of entertainment in both court circles and the private salons of the well-to-do.[11] One of the most renowned talents of the day was Ibrahim's own sister 'Ulayyah to whom he was greatly devoted.

It was this milieu that shaped Ibrahim's childhood and youth. By temperament an artist, he excelled in music and poetry.[12] Maintaining cordial relations with all factions at the court, he nevertheless kept aloof of political intrigue. Although appointed by Harun governor of Damascus for two brief periods, Ibrahim's experience there ill equipped him for the turmoil which engulfed the Abbasid realm after Harun's death. Civil war erupted between Harun's designated joint successors, his sons al-Amin and al-Ma'mun. When al-Amin was killed, Ibrahim was elevated to the Caliphal throne as a figurehead of the anti-al-Ma'mun faction in Baghdad. For two years he struggled ineffectually to cope with a deteriorating situation against superior forces. Finally, upon al-Ma'mun's triumphal entry into Baghdad, Ibrahim prudently fled his nephew's wrath. With a price on his head, he spent the next four (some say six) years hiding out somewhere in the capital or its environs. In the popular lore of the day a glimpse is caught of the fugitive moving about the quarters of Baghdad in disguise. But eventually he was caught and imprisoned. Al-Ma'mun in the end forgave his uncle and extended to him the honour of becoming his court companion, or *nadim*. To Ibrahim's relief he was able to resume his life among the more familiar and secure circle of poets and singers. He survived into the reign of al-Ma'mun's successor, al-Mu'tasim (another of Harun's sons to whom a cookbook is also attributed) and died, aged sixty, in 225/839. The Caliph honoured his uncle by reciting the oration at the funeral.

Ibrahim's gourmet tastes appear to have developed while he was still a young man. The prince himself recounts his inviting Harun for dinner one evening. The Caliph's custom was to commence his meal with hot dishes followed by a number of cold plates called *bawarid*. As these latter were placed on the table, Harun noticed one plate containing what appeared to be a fish cut up into minute pieces. He enquired why the cook had chopped the fish into such fine, tiny bits. The 'bits', Ibrahim informed him, were in fact more than one hundred and fifty fish tongues created in a fish's shape. Harun asked the cost of the dish. Ibrahim replied, 'More than 1000 dirhems.' Harun chastised Ibrahim for his foolish prodigality. As a gesture of penance he ordered a similar amount to be distributed among the poor. And to Ibrahim's great chagrin, Harun also ordered the platter upon which the fish had been served to be given to the first passer-by in the street. The platter, purchased by Ibrahim to honour his brother, had cost him several times more than the fish tongues alone![13]

Yet Harun was not unsympathetic to the culinary arts, despite the impression this anecdote might convey. We know of many dishes that he was fond of in particular and one, a meat preparation cooked in sumac juice, which was named after him. Moreover, Harun held his brother in esteem and affection. He even encouraged Ibrahim's interests in gourmandise by bestowing upon him a gift of rare value. Recalling him from the governorship of Damascus, Harun presented Ibrahim with a slave girl, named Badi'a. This remarkable woman was said to have been the most highly skilled and discerning person in the art of cooking. Her specialities included *bawarid* dishes[14] and sweetmeats.

Ibrahim was enchanted. Badi'a remained with him for many years, for we find her during the reign of al-Amin, preparing for the Caliph at Ibrahim's behest, an old favourite of the Sassanian Persian court, *sikbaj*.[15] Fortuitously, a fruitful relationship had developed between prince and concubine, the gourmand and the cook, whose collaboration it doubtless was that led to the creation of Ibrahim's cookbook, *Kitab al-Tabikh*, the first of its kind of Arabic.

Following his sojourn in Damascus, Ibrahim took up residence in his own palace situated in the quarter called the Market of Thirst, *Suq al-'Atsh*, on the upper east side of Baghdad. The palace was near the Main Bridge leading across the Tigris to the original round City of Peace. Nearby, too, his pleasure boat was moored. A quiet jaunt on the river made a welcome diversion from the intrusions of palace life and the city's crowded and noisy streets. On board, Ibrahim could enjoy a game of chess with Harun or entertain a few companions to a session of poetry and song accompanied by food and drink. Pleasure boats were a common sight on the river, their crews moving them sedately through the crush of hundreds of craft of every shape and size to the quieter reaches of the river above and below the city.

The river also gave easy access by boat to those immensely popular places of gathering, the gardens and vineyards of the Christian monasteries.[16] On feast days, as on other occasions, Christians and Muslims, men and women, mingled to enjoy an outing in the soothing shade of the riverside. These outings were self-catering picnics, wine probably being supplied for those who so desired from the monasteries' own production. Picnic fare lost little from that served at the household table. Meat, or meat and vegetable dishes, prepared in advance and transported in containers could be reheated over a portable brazier; the numerous kinds of *bawarid* made from vegetables, meat, fish or fowl, provided excellent, delicate accompaniment. Fresh fish caught from the river could be roasted on the spot and served with prepared sauces (*sibagh*).[17] Fresh fruit completed the meal. For the urban dweller perhaps the picnic was a kind of nostalgic re-enactment of the Beduin encampment so often depicted in early Arabic odes.

We do not know when Ibrahim conceived his cookbook. It undoubtedly reflected the many evenings' entertainment in the palace, in the salons of his friends, or during convivial picnic days. Food and drink were no mere adornment of these assemblies at which poetry, music, story telling and debate on literary and political topics were of common and consuming interest. Food itself was a topic of discussion in both a literary and an edible fashion. Ibrahim composed a number of poems on food, such as one on the delights of salt, and certain recipes he even cast in poetic form.[18] In this very personal manner of expression, Ibrahim reveals his intimate acquaintance with the techniques and processes of cooking. If not the actual innovator of the culinary poem, he was certainly its most prominent early exponent, his influence even touching later famous poets like Ibn al-Rumi (d. 283/896) and the Abbasid poet-prince Ibn al-Mu'tazz (d. 296/908).

From the surviving fragments of Ibrahim's cookbook, some forty-odd recipes, it is evident that it was intended to be comprehensive in coverage, from a bread-like preparation, to many substantial main dishes, cold plates and sweetmeats. Three preparations for the well-known dish called *zirbaj* have come down to us.[19] This was a kind of 'sweet-sour' meat dish with vinegar and dried fruit or sugar as the main flavour ingredients. Ibrahim's different preparations reveal not only subtle nuanced variations but also the gastronome's own empirical or innovative approach to cooking. He was also apparently intrigued by the 'green revolution' vegetable, the eggplant or aubergine. Three recipes which highlight it are again quite different from each other, although each is a cold preparation (*bawarid*).[20] There are also two recipes for a dish featuring the turnip, called *Shaljamiya*, and two for a fried meat dish called *al-mutajjan*.[21] Among the recipes included in this present volume of adaptations is one called *al-mutajjan al-Ibrahimiya*, from a later seventh/thirteenth century cookbook compiled in Baghdad at the very end of the Abbasid period; the dish is named in honour of the great master. His memory was celebrated even further afield than his native Baghdad. A chapter of recipes attributed to Ibrahim is to be found in an anonymous work of Moroccan and Andalusian cooking. The recipes, however, may only be loosely related to Ibrahim's actual cookbook and be adaptations of a subsequent generation and locale.

In the sophisticated circles of Baghdadi society, a knowledge of the culinary arts was not the exclusive possession of a cadre of professional cooks. In no small measure it was the influence of Ibrahim and the like-minded gastronomes of his day who impressed upon their own and subsequent generations, the public pleasures to be derived from what essentially was a private craft; the 'new wave' gastronome, as we have styled him, far removed from what today would be called a cookery writer, although his interests were by no means casual or superficial. It is, however, impossible to say how widespread was the use of cookbooks. Certainly there existed a lively trade in manuscript copying by persons who also acted as booksellers, and in such fashion all manner of knowledge was disseminated, including culinary. The earliest collection of recipes to come down to us was compiled in the late fourth/tenth century by one Abu Muhammad al-Muzaffar ibn Nasr ibn Sayyar al-Warraq. He was able to employ manuscript copies of culinary works, including Ibrahim's, made during the first half of the previous century. And, as his name al-Warraq suggests, he was both copyist and seller of his own reproductions. Thus the informally combined efforts of the gastronome and the bookseller caused questions of food and drink to become an accepted part of the developing urban high culture. These concerns are mirrored in the encyclopaedias of socially useful knowledge like the *'Uyun al-Akhbar* of Ibn Qutayba and the *'Iqd al-Farid* of Ibn 'Abd Rabbihi.

The literary expression of an haute cuisine was perpetuated in Baghdad throughout the remainder of the third/ninth century and well into the next. Only the names of these second or third generation authors/compilers are known as none of their recipe collections is extant even in fragmentary form. After al-Warraq's collection, it is not until the seventh/thirteenth century that another recipe book of Iraqi provenance is found, which has survived to the present day. Compiled by one Muhammad ibn al-Hasan ibn Muhammad ibn Karim al-Katib al-Baghdadi, nothing of substance is known about him. In the preface to his cookbook al-Baghdadi expresses an enthusiasm for good eating but perhaps with a certain loss of his predecessors' broader vision which included good food as but a part of the whole of cultured life. He says, 'I subscribe to the doctrine of the pre-excellence of the pleasure of eating above all other pleasures.'[22] Nevertheless, his recipes, which form the second major source for the adaptations in this volume, display features of both continuity, in the repertoire of methods, and change, in the introduction of new ingredients, over against earlier periods.

The influence of the 'new wave' generation quickly extended beyond Baghdad itself to other urban centres of the empire. The Caliphal capital imposed not only its literary but its culinary fashions as well upon the provinces. And, in one instance, the influence of Ibrahim can be inferred as having been direct. The historian Ibn al-Daya, who became a functionary at the Tulunid court in Cairo also wrote a cookery book; his father had been the secretary and foster brother of Ibrahim ibn al-Mahdi.[23]

It is now time to set aside these reflections upon the culinary history of the early Abbasids and enter the kitchen of a prosperous and well provisioned household of the period. The recipes themselves will provide a guide to the techniques, processes and ingredients of the urban high cooking tradition.

Portrait of a medieval kitchen[24]

The kitchen has been described as the 'birthplace' and the 'foster home' of innumerable terms, operations and apparatuses in the very early stage of man's development of technology. The techniques of crushing or disintegration, of fermentation, the methods of preservation of perishable organic material and the oven all reveal their origin in the preparation of food. The technology and chemistry of cooking were thus realms of practical knowledge which the Islamic world inherited from the ancient centres of Middle Eastern civilization in Iraq and Egypt. The inheritance was not, however, shared equally by all segments of the population: techniques which had perhaps originated or been refined in the kitchens of the ancient temple and the palace were appropriated by the medieval urban cook, whereas the rural and nomadic populations retained the more primitive methods of food preparation.

A simple example will illustrate this rural-urban contrast. Bread making is an activity common to all. The Swiss traveller, J.L. Burckhardt observed the following method among the Beduin of the Arabian peninsula in the 1830 s. First, a circular 'element' of stones was heated, wherever the encampment of the tribe happened to be located. Then the fire was removed and dough made from coarse ground grain was set on the stones over which the glowing ashes were placed until the bread was cooked. The result was a round, rather hard, unleavened loaf.[25]

Bread made in a prosperous medieval household was, by contrast, baked in its own kitchen from the very best ingredients. The appliance used was the *tannur*, of ancient Mesopotamian origin. Cylindrical, bee-hive shaped, it gave the appearance of a large, inverted pot from which it probably had evolved. Fuel, preferably good charcoal, was inserted through a side opening, ignited, and when the oven was sufficiently hot, baking could commence. The oven's temperature could to some extent be regulated by closing the various appertures. The loaf, made from fine white wheat, could come in a number of shapes, sizes and textures. Many implements associated with bread making are mentioned in the Arabic sources: a dough board (*lawh*), a small rolling pin (*shawbaq*) for the ordinary loaf (*raghif*), and a large one for the thin loaf (*riqaq*). A feather for coating the dough in certain preparations, a wooden bowl (*jafna*) in which the dough was mixed and a metal scraper (*mihaqq*) for cleaning it. Yeast was kept in a wooden container called a *mihlab*. A cloth (*mandil*) was used to wipe the unbaked loaf and another for wiping down the oven to remove unwanted moisture or condensation.

A poker (*sinnara*) was used to remove the loaf from the oven if it fell onto the oven floor, and a metal instrument (*mihraq*) for raking out the embers and ash from the oven when baking was completed. Altogether a lengthier and more complicated process of bread making than that employed by the beduin!

The concept and design of the medieval domestic kitchen in Baghdad probably owed much to Mesopotamian inspiration which survived down to the last remaining examples of the open courtyard house in the modern day Iraqi capital. The kitchen (*matbakh*) in multi-courtyard dwellings was a whole complex comprising the kitchen proper, opening onto its own courtyard with adjoining ancillary areas such as store rooms, toilet and bathroom, a well, and possibly a cook's room. The upper part of the courtyard, level with the first floor of the house was surrounded by blank walls and open to the sky. The kitchen of a single courtyard house faced directly onto the courtyard itself and had either fewer or no ancillary areas attached to it. Larger multi-courtyard houses might have a second kitchen adjacent to the rooms where guests were entertained. The palaces of the Caliphs and of the Abbasid princes were doubtless fashioned on a much larger scale but along essentially similar lines.

Inside the kitchen again, the *tannur* was not used exclusively for baking bread. A recipe for a kind of chicken pie made in a pan (*miqla*) is described as being lowered into the oven to cook. Another dish, a meat, rice and vegetable casserole made in a pot (*qidr*) was placed in the oven to finish cooking. Both of these preparations were, not surprisingly, called oven-dishes, *tannuriya*. Often they might be left to stew overnight in a slowly cooling oven to be served the following day.

The second major cooking contrivance found in a well equipped kitchen was known simply as the 'fire-place', *mustawqid*. This was designed to accommodate several cooking pots and/or pans side by side at the same time. It was erected to about half a person's height giving easy access to the food and was provided with vents allowing for an intake of air and for the expulsion of smoke.

Households which possessed neither adequate kitchen space, equipment nor labour for large meals, could resort to the services of the neighourhood or communal oven, the *furn*. In this case, the initial stages of preparation of a dish would be made at home and then taken to the *furn* for cooking. The communal oven would also cater to any household's requirements on festive occasions. Affluent households might also hire the specialist skills of a sweetmeat maker.

The *batterie de cuisine* comprised a range of other utensils. Cooking pots made of stone, earthenware, copper or lead came in various sizes. Pans generally used for frying fish and the like were made of iron. Other implements were roasting skewers (*saffud*), a copper basin (*nuqra*) for washing smaller containers and vessels in hot water, a copper rod-like instrument (*mihashsh*) for stuffing intestines, a large knife for jointing and smaller ones for cutting up vegetables. There were several kinds of strainer (*misfa*) made of wood or metal, a ladle (*mighrafa*) and a mallet (*midrab*). Spices were crushed or powdered in a mortar (*hawun*) and kept in glass vessels. A similar, but larger stone mortar (*jawun*) was used for pounding meat or crushing vegetables. Meat was cut up on a wooden table (*khiwan*). Sweetmeats required another set of utensils, especially the moulds (*qawalib*) as frequently these dishes were served in the shape of a fish or bird. Food preparation involved a set of activities which were labour intensive and time consuming. Unfortunately, we do not possess data on the day-to-day details of kitchen management, especially concerning the personnel, the cook and his or her assistants, a chief steward and so on. There is, however, clear evidence that kitchen management was taken very seriously to ensure that all cooking pans and utensils were kept clean to prevent food from spoiling. Al-Baghdadi's instructions in the preface of his cookbook urges that 'the utmost care be taken when washing the utensils used in cooking and the saucepans; let them be rubbed with brick dust, then with dry powdered potash and saffron and finally with a fresh leaf of citron.' The opening chapter of al-Warraq's cookbook deals with means of avoiding food contamination. Meat must be thoroughly cleaned of any blood and washed in pure cold water in a clean bowl; a knife used to cut up vegetables should not be used at the same time for slicing up meat; spices which are old, have lost their essential flavour and become bitter should not be used lest they 'corrupt the pot'. Likewise salt and oil should be tasted before adding them to cooking food checking whether their condition is still sound. Attention must be paid to see that the liquid of stews or bits of onion have not dried on the inside of pots and so spoil the food when they are next used.

Finally, the kitchen or kitchen complex was the scene of operations other than those devoted to the immediate preparation of meals. Indeed the word kitchen (*matbakh*) comes from a common root in the Semitic family of languages which means 'the cooking of flesh meat' and also 'slaughtering'. It was common enough for a sheep or goat and several fowl to inhabit the kitchen yard awaiting their destiny in the cooking pot. Thus meat was kept and cooked fresh. Fruits, herbs and certain vegetables were also dried and placed in store for future use. Pickled vegetables or special condiments, such as *murri*, which required several weeks to prepare were also put in store, along with home made beer and wine. The wide range of activities associated with the transformation of food from its 'raw' to 'cooked' state are all reflected in the treasury of contemporary recipes. The kitchen and its proper management was of central importance to the smooth running of the family household's daily life; but also important were the broader social and political aspects of food preparation and consumption, which were equally dependent upon the successful functioning of this most crucial patch of domestic space.

Food preparation: ingredients and processes

The vast majority of recipes in the medieval Arabic treasury contained meat of some kind, whether flesh of mammal, fish or poultry. But there was also an expressed preference for particular kinds of meat. Recipes for other than fish and fowl use only the word 'meat' (*lahm*). Appearing alone and unqualified it should be assumed that mutton is intended, the urban dweller's first preference and a choice supported by favourable opinion among the fraternity of physicians.

Medieval Middle Eastern taste was, in this respect, rather closer to that of Victorians who felt that sheep should be killed between three to five years 'at which age the mutton will be firm and succulent, dark coloured and full of the richest gravy.' Today tastes have changed. Moreover, since fine mutton, raised to eat, is expensive and difficult to obtain, the modernized versions of recipes in this volume call for lamb. Medieval Arabic is rich in terms for livestock, depending on the age and sex of the animal or on how many young a female has borne. It is impossible to determine at what age they preferred to eat their mutton, as hoggets (between one and two years) or older. Meat which was too old was deemed tough and therefore bad for digestion. The widespread preference for mutton over the centuries is illustrated in a somewhat curious and unexpected manner. The meat diet of the Roman army of occupation in Britain was chiefly beef and pork. In two places, however, Barr Hill fort on the Antoinine Wall and Corbridge in Northumberland, a very high proportion of mutton bones was found among the site remains. Both locations had been manned by Syrian or other oriental units of the Roman army, homesick foreigners compensating for long absence from their distant homeland.[26]

The medieval gourmand regarded kid meat (*jadi*) more highly even than lamb. Physicians recommended it as suitable for persons of ease and comfort because of its natural balance between the four elements of heat, cold, wetness and dryness. Beef, on the other hand, owing to its coarseness, was judged better for those who laboured and toiled. Lean 'red' meat was preferred to fat meat. The physicians' views, adopted from Greek cosmography and medical theory, did not perhaps decisively influence the eating habits of the medieval urbanite in these specific instances; it was more likely a matter of borrowed theory rationalizing existing practice.

In Baghdad, on both sides of the river, butchers' markets located in special quarters sold freshly killed meat or meat 'on the hoof', for slaughter in the household kitchen. A preparation called *hallam* describes the steps for slaughtering a young animal and boiling in vinegar the jointed carcass in its skin until it was cooked. The meat was then left overnight in a mixture of vinegar, cinnamon, galingal, thyme, celery, quince, citron and salt and then stored for future use in glass or earthenware containers. An additional advantage of buying a live animal was that every part could be used in the widest variety of dishes, from the pickling process noted here to the preparation of offal in which the eyes, tongue, and brain were much valued. The kidneys, liver, heart, intestines, trotters and stomach were also eaten.

Of game, rabbit (which was also raised domestically), hare, wild cow, wild ass, and especially gazelle are found in the medieval culinary repertoire; horse, mountain goat, oryx, and stag were also considered edible. The cooking of game animals seems particularly associated with the 'water and salt' (*al-ma' wa'l-milh*) process, well suited to cooking in the open after the hunt or in the kitchen. Large chunks of the animal were first boiled to 'firm' the meat. The water was then discarded, the excess moisture squeezed out and the meat added to fresh water and oil and a 'handful' of salt together with onions, cinnamon, galingal and dill. Game meat was also cut up into thin strips, spiced and hung to dry (called *qadid*) a method similar to the biltong of the South African pioneers in their trek northwards from the Cape. In this manner and in salted form (*namaksud*) game meat reached the markets of Baghdad.

Fowl ranked among the most important food resources in the kitchen. The domestic chicken was of several varieties but the Kaskari, named after a district in Iraq, was especially noted for its superb taste and plumpness; it was reputed to grow to the weight of a young lamb. The gastronome of Baghdad with a penchant for hunting had the good fortune that in spring and autumn large numbers of birds passed through Iraq either on the way to their breeding haunts further north or to their winter quarters in Africa. The country also possessed an abundance of indigenous species of fowl hunted by all classes of society. Game birds of every size and variety, from the grouse, pheasant, francolin to the bustard, quail, partridge, crane, ostrich and heron all found their way into the kitchen and onto the table.

The main cooking techniques for dishes containing animal flesh or fowl, reflect principles described by the famous modern French chef Michael Guerard. One of these he calls cooking by exchange. This consists of first sautéing meat pieces briskly in hot oil to retain their juices and nutritive elements. The medieval cook would, by preference, have used sesame (*shiraj*) or olive oil, although sheep tail fat was widely used as well. Then the meat is moistened with water to half its depth or more. Seasonings may be added at either this or the first stage, frequently at both. Other ingredients, vegetables, dried fruit or cheese may be added according to the type of dish. The juices sealed inside the meat are gradually released to combine with the cooking liquid and at the same time the meat absorbs and is enriched by the various flavours of the liquid itself. Hence the 'exchange'. An example of this technique will be found in the recipe for *Isfanakhiya*.[27]

Guerard calls his second general law cooking by sealing, where the juices and nutriments are imprisoned inside the cooking meat. It is used in grilling, sautéing and frying. The recipe for *Mutajjan bi sadr al-dajjaj*[28] is an example of this. A combination of these two principles seems to be found in the recipe for *Zirbaj*. Here the meat is first boiled in a seasoned stock of water and oil to which other ingredients are later added while the cooking time is brought slowly to an end.

Dishes like those called *Zirbaj* demonstrate the widespread culinary custom of meat substitution. The main characteristic of *Zirbaj* was sweet and sour flavour provided generally by vinegar and some sweetening agent. Yet recipes for this dish call at times for 'meat', i.e. lamb, at other times fowl, or even a combination of the two. The practice can still be found today, for example, in the cooking of North Africa.

While it would be true to say that the new cuisine was most heavily influenced by Persian cooking traditions, other traditions were not insignificant. The ancient Mesopotamian is as yet the most indistinct; rather than the survival of particular dishes, it is the food resources indigenous to Iraq (for example, wheat and barley, the pea, lentil, pistachio and so on) which formed part of this heritage. The Arab tradition is far more apparent. Dishes like *Sawiq* and *Tharid*, well known at the time of the Prophet Muhammad, found their way into the new cuisine, albeit transformed by the use of more expensive ingredients. *Sawiq* was parched barley meal which, when prepared, required reconstitution with water or milk and was suitable as basic nourishment on long journeys. A dish of this name was sold in the markets of Baghdad as a poor man's staple made from powdered chick peas. In affluent households, this rustic preparation was made from fine wheat flour sweetened with sugar or mixed with other ingredients like pomegranate seeds. *Tharid* was celebrated in a tradition from the Prophet who exclaimed that it was the most excellent of foods just as his wife A'isha was the most excellent of women. This simple traditional Arab fare consisted of diced meat cooked in broth with dried bread crumbled over it during the last stage of cooking. This dish likewise became transformed in the urban high cooking tradition, made from lamb, or kid, or beef or chicken, together with various vegetables but always with pieces of bread broken over it. Ibrahim's recipes for *Masliya* and *Madira*[29] also point to the Arab cooking tradition, in their use of milk products; *Masliya* contains the dried whey of curd cheese (*masl*) while *Madira* is a dish of meat cooked in soured milk.

Pig flesh is notable by its absence in the recipe collections, witness to the fact that the cuisine was part of Islamic culture. There are few religious food taboos in Islam, those there are being based in the main upon the Koranic passage. 'These things only has He forbidden you: carrion, blood, the flesh of swine and what has been hallowed to other than God'. The Jewish communities of the Middle East equally observed the prohibition of pig's flesh, although the Christian population was under no such constraint.

The great twin rivers of the Tigris and Euphrates, their tributaries, the swamp region of their lower reaches bordering the Arab Gulf, and the inland lakes of Iraq all provided ample sources of fish. The fresh water varieties were likely dominated by the carp family (*Cyprinidae*). Marine species invaded the lower Tigris from the Gulf as did species which migrated into fresh waters to breed and feed. Large fish were regarded as the most nourishing and some reached weights of two to three hundred pounds. Fish of the Tigris were deemed better than those of the Euphrates; the commonly held Iraqi view was that fish from either source was in any case more delicious than fish from the Nile. Dishes were prepared from fresh or salted fish, and fried, soused (*mamqur*) or roasted.[30] Ibrahim's early fancy for fish tongues is not, unfortunately, expressed in the surviving fragment of his cookbook! He was of the opinion that fish should be accompanied by a relish and his recipe for *Sibagh* is one such preparation.[31]

*   *   *

Vegetables (*buqul*) were said, by those of cultivated taste, to be 'ornaments of the table'. And, as the Arabic proverb went, 'A table without vegetables is like an old man without wisdom.' The wide range of vegetables available from one season to another were prepared in a variety of ways, as cold plates like Ibrahim's preparation with aubergine,[32] in hot meat casseroles, and in relishes. Along with the usual vegetables like leeks, carrots, turnip and spinach the term *buqul* included other plants such as mint, garlic, coriander, dill and so on. Fruits (*fawaqih*) were classified as fresh and dried. Of the fresh variety, the most common was the date, the food of rich and poor alike, of which there were more than three hundred kinds. Dried fruit included soft fruit like apples, pears, apricots and peaches as well as nuts such as almonds, walnuts, pine seeds and hazelnuts.

Meat dishes have already been remarked upon above. Many other preparations also contained meat but were considered primarily as vegetable or fruit dishes and were known by the name of the particular fruit or vegetable highlighted in them. Thus *Shaljamiya* is a turnip dish, *Isfanakhiya*, a spinach dish, *Mishmishiya*[33] an apricot dish and and *Tuffahiya*,[34] a dish made with apples. Other plant foods classified as 'seeds' or 'grains' (*hubub*) were used in many dishes: these included the chick pea, lentils (and hence the dish called '*Adasiya*),[35] beans and peas. The grasses wheat, barley and rice also featured in main dishes (see the recipe for the rice dish, *Aruzziya*).[36] It will be remarked that a quality of sourness is common to many of these dishes, imparted by either vinegar or lemon or grape juice. The tangy nature of these ingredients had to be blunted or offset by a balance of sweetness which was provided by sugar or honey, or by a combination of other ingredients in the dish. The highest grade of sugar was called Tabarzad, made from the reed stem of cane sugar; boiled three times to remove all impurities, it was solidified and had to be broken into small pieces for cooking. Less pure kinds of sugar were called Sulaimani and red sugar. Acids could also be tempered by ground almonds, chick peas, or rice, all of which acted as thickening agents for the stock. The aim always was to create harmony among the contrasting flavours in the dish.

The common style of preparation of all these meat or vegetable dishes was stewing the contents slowly over the fire in pots with lip-edged rims which could be fitted with lids. These casserole dishes are common today throughout the Middle East, although baking sometimes replaces the stewing process, and are found under various names such as *Yakhni, Khurish* and *Tajin.* Certain Turkish *Pilavs* may be included as well. The combinations of meat, vegetables, fruits, and nuts were endless.

As in the case of medieval Chinese literature, it is not possible to identify precisely in every case, the variety of every plant, its English name or scientific term, used in cooking. A vegetable like the leek is sometimes simply referred to in recipes as *kurrath*, sometimes as Greek *(kurrath Rumi)* or else Nabatean *(kurrath Nabati).* Likewise celery may be mentioned in an unqualified sense, *karafs*, or else as a wild, garden or mountain variety; to complicate matters, wild celery *(karafs barri)* could also mean wild caraway. It is uncertain whether a vegetable like the turnip which had more than one name *(shaljam* and *lift)* meant the same or different varieties. The same Arabic word might also refer to two different, although related, vegetables; *qunnabit*, for example, could be either cauliflower or broccoli, while *kurumb* might be either cauliflower or cabbage. Moreover, there were regional names for the same plant and disputes arose as to which name appropriately applied to which plant.

Vegetable plants in particular were held to have generative or inhibiting powers over certain bodily functions. The following views derived from contemporary medical wisdom were commonplace. Rocket *(gargir)* was supposed to increase the sexual appetite and the flow of one's urine. Rue *(sadhab)* on the other hand reduced sexual desire. Moreover, if a pregnant woman were to eat a certain quantity of rue mixed in hot water or wine for twenty-five days, she would abort. The word comes from the Greek *ruta* to 'set free', indicating its medical properties, but in large quantities it was toxic. The chick pea *(himmas)* was multi-purposed: apart from increasing the sexual appetite, it would cause sperms to multiply, increase a suckling mother's milk and would cause a woman's menstrual blood to flow abundantly. There were antidotes to most of these properties of plant food, the permutations in the construction of a theoretically sound diet becoming almost infinite. Physicians advice on the virtues and complex effects of various foods on persons of different 'temperaments' undoubtedly was based on much common sense and tried tradition; some views, on the other hand, were based on superstition. Nevertheless, there was flexibility in the medico-culinary system of the medieval Arabs, permitting the gourmet to enjoy his favourite dish, whatever its indications were for his particular constitution.

*   *   *

Much ingenuity was exercised in devising the myriad pleasing ways to transform the raw food resources of the kitchen into the kaleidoscope of flavours, textures and aromas produced at the table. Unlike a recipe in today's cookbook, reflecting the precision of our so-called scientific age, the medieval recipe by comparison belonged more to the world of the artist who was offered a sketch to guide him to the creation of a dish of individual distinction. The medieval Arabic recipe was precise as to the process of creation, but completely non-committal as to the measures and proportions of the constituent ingredients. The creative core of the cuisine was the cook's intuitive use of herbs and spices, of condiments and relishes which accompanied the main dishes or else were used to season them during cooking. Balance and harmony among the herbs and spices used in a dish was important, the particular categories being referred to as substances which were either 'aromatic' or 'pungent'. The former group included the following: musk, ambergrise ('*anbar*), rosewater, saffron, cinnamon (*dar sini*), galingal (*khulanjan*), clove, mastic (*mastika*), nutmeg (*jawz bawwa*), mace (*bisbasa*) and ginger. The latter category of 'pungent' substances included the very common pepper, long pepper (*dar filfil*), cumin, dried coriander, which may have meant the dried leaves as well as the seeds, caraway, lovage (*kashim*), asafetida (*hiltit*), thyme and vinegar. Salt was very important, the best variety being obtained from the evaporation of sea water and called *andarani*; as the Arabic adage had it, 'Salt is as necessary in food as grammar is in speech.'

Within the broad spice spectrum there were, not surprisingly, particular favourites. An interesting feature is revealed from a content comparison of the seasonings used in two seventh/thirteenth century cookbooks, one of Iraqi provenance and the other of North African origin. In the Iraqi cookbook, which is that of al-Baghdadi, the most commonly used seasonings in descending order of frequency are cinnamon, coriander, cumin, mastic and pepper (with saffron a little way behind), while in the latter work the order is pepper, coriander, cinnamon, and saffron (with cumin somewhat behind). Does this comparison reflect actual regional differences or perhaps only the preferences of the individual compiler of each cookbook? No answer can be conclusive. Nevertheless, the balance in bouquet and flavour between cinnamon and coriander may be said to be the characteristic heart of the spice spectrum used in medieval Middle Eastern cuisine. The essential oils of cinnamon and, say pepper, were known for their antiseptic, preservative, properties. However, since meat could be cooked freshly slaughtered there was probably little need to mask the smell or taste of rotting food with distinctively pungent or aromatic spices. The use of spices with preservative properties, therefore, was likely as much a matter of aesthetics, the preservative function being useful when leftovers could be served the following day with the flavour of the dish enhanced. It was the 'spice spectrum' which Europe inherited from the Middle East and which transformed much of European cuisine from the fourteenth century onward.

The spice spectrum points to the cuisine's complexity as well as to its cost. Many of the pungent seasonings had been known for centuries in the Middle East, thyme, coriander and cumin among them. It was chiefly the aromatic spices such as cloves, cinnamon, ginger and nutmeg which were imported from the East, from India, Tibet and China; the pungent pepper was obtained from the same sources. These reached Baghdad by overland caravan and by sea and were consequently highly prized and expensive. The round trip by sea from the Arab Gulf to China was some 16,000 kilometres of hazardous travel. Merchants' gains from the trade made a successful journey highly profitable, so much so that the temptation was great to adulterate the spices. Thus top quality, pure spices, commanded the most exorbitant prices. The ability to purchase them was also a mark of status; one bureaucrat was prompted to boast that in his household he ground saffron as other people ground their bread flour. It was probably during the early Abbasid period that expensive aromatics began to be extensively employed, imparting new flavours to the many regional dishes being incorporated into the new cuisine.

The preservation of foodstuffs by pickling was an operation carried out in the domestic kitchen. The preparation *hallam* of a whole kid or lamb has already been noted. Another, called *mamqur* was for chicken lightly cooked whole in water, salt and oil, then jointed and the portions placed in a jar filled with vinegar and seasonings. When it was to be used, the meat was fried and served. It is worth mentioning in passing that the vinegar employed in the medieval kitchen was genuine *vin aigre* or soured wine, just as the term *khall khamar* indicates. Vinegar was also used in the preservation of a wide variety of *mukhallalat*, pickled fare, made from among other ingredients, onions, capers, cucumber, turnip, garlic, aubergine and mint.[37] These plates were served during meals in order, as al-Baghdadi says, 'to cleanse the palate of greasiness, to appetize, to assist the digestion, and to stimulate the banqueter.'[38]

As varied as the pickle preparations were relishes or condiments known by the general term *kawamikh*. They were served, several at a time, in small bowls into which bread or morsels of food could be dipped. Certain types of *kamakh* or *kamakh* juice were used as seasoning and added to the cooking pot. Their preparation was often time consuming, requiring almost daily attention for a period from between six to twelve weeks. One basic ingredient, called *budhaj*, was made from wheat or barley loaves wrapped in fig leaves and left for forty days to become dried out and slightly turned. Then a powdered portion of this and four portions of dried, powdered unleavened bread blended together with a handful of salt was worked into a doughy substance by adding fresh milk. Placed in a container, the mixture was left in the sun throughout the summer's heat, milk added as required and the contents stirred twice daily until firmly set. To this *kamakh* base cloves, cinnamon, caraway or other spices could be added to yield clove or cinnamon or caraway *kamakh*. Not all of these preparations were as tortuous to make. The recipe for olives which appears in Ibrahim's repertoire is simplicity itself.[39]

Another ingredient frequently mentioned in the medieval recipes is *murri*. This was a prepared seasoning of considerable antiquity. It has been erroneously identified with *garum* which in the Roman culinary tradition was a generic name for fish essence. *Murri* on the other hand, as the few extant recipes show, was made from cereal grain, barley and wheat. Throughout the three-month long process of preparation, quantities of dried bread were added to a vessel containing a seasoned solution of oil and water sufficient to allow the mixture to be stirred every day. Towards the end of the process the 'must' was strained off and stored in jars sealed with oil while the 'lees' were left a further two weeks, stirred daily, and then strained and bottled. The colour of this residual *murri* was black, its flavour bitter. Sumac is suggested as a substitute for *murri* in one recipe; they may have been similar in their bitterness, as the astringency of sumac is due to the organic acids (malic, gallic, and tannic) in its composition. In any event only small quantities of *murri* would have been required in a given dish.

Scented salt was, like the *kamakh* preparations, used both as a seasoning in cooking food and as a condiment at the table. To salt were added the following: sumac, pomegranate seeds, asafetida, sesame and cumin.

The condiments (*kawamikh*) and the cold dishes (*bawarid*) of the medieval table strongly suggest the origin of the modern Middle Eastern *mezza*. In today's cookbooks *mezza* is loosely translated as hors d'oeuvres. Yet, accompanied as they should be by the anise drink *arak*, a water pipe, good company and plenty of time, the almost limitless variety of *mezza* dishes can be enjoyed as an entire meal in itself. A *mezza* dish is the modern equivalent of a small portion of a medieval condiment or cold plate. It is interesting too that the important notion of harmony (of flavours, but also of textures and colour) has survived down the centuries, for one of the medieval connotations of the root meaning of the word *mezza* is the taste of something halfway between sweet and sour.

*　　*　　*

Notwithstanding religious injunctions against intoxicating beverages, they were consumed in most segments of society, except by those who viewed religious commandments with solemn gravity. Recipes are extant for a kind of barley beer called *Fuqqa'* which could be simply and cheaply made. By mixing into the basic barley wort ingredients such as wheat, rice or walnuts, the flavour and consistency were altered. A more exotic type was brewed from barley sweetened with honey and seasoned with pepper, cloves, ginger, cinnamon and rue with a handful of millet (*jawars*) blended in. Fermentation was achieved by placing the contents in a skin container (*kir*) and leaving it for two days ready for drinking on the third. Wine (*nabidh*) was prepared in several ways. One version was made with honey and raisins which, judging from the recipe, was a lawful, i.e. unfermented, brew. Another kind was decidedly of the forbidden variety, a honey wine fermented for forty days and then bottled for four months before drinking.

In its broadest sense the word *sharab*, beverage, denotes any liquid regardless of its consistency. The word could apply to thick syrups made by boiling and greatly reducing a particular flavoured liquid. Beet leaf syrup, for example, was prepared by first squeezing the juice from the leaves and boiling one part juice with one part honey, reducing the liquid by half before adding cloves, cinnamon, spikenard and nutmeg. The syrup was stored in flasks until ready for use. Sweet and sour syrups were made from honey boiled with the extracted juice of sour apples, quinces, pomegranates, pears and plums. From the culinary sources it is unclear as to the precise use these syrups were put. They may have been drunk diluted and chilled or else used to flavour the stock in which certain vegetables were cooked, or as flavouring for salad dressings in much the same way as pomegranate syrup is employed in the Middle East today.

Here is the point at which we must bring to an end this sojourn through the culinary world of the medieval Middle East. To Ibrahim ibn al-Mahdi and his numerous, often anonymous, successors, the historian is greatly indebted. Without their efforts at collecting, experimenting and recording, without good fortune which assured the survival of at least some of their work, the world library of medieval culinary knowledge would be sadly impoverished.

Of gourmandism the nineteenth century philosopher of the kitchen, Brillat-Savarin, remarked that it inspired both 'the efforts which every good host must make to entertain his guests and the gratitude of his guests when they see what pains have been taken on their behalf.' To which he solemnly added that one must 'cry eternal shame on those stupid eaters who swallow the choicest dainties with culpable indifference, or breathe in with sacrilegious insouciance the fragrance of a limpid nectar.' In the mind's eye one can imagine Ibrahim nodding approval of the sentiment. As he gave to Arab culture its first cookbook over a millenium ago, so now the modern gourmet is offered the opportunity of recreating these adventures in the kitchen.

Notes

1 The two works chiefly employed are the *Kitab al-Tabikh* by Ibn Sayyar al-Warraq, edited by Kaj Ohrnberg and Sahban Mroueh, Helsinki (1987) and the *Kitab al-Tabikh* by Muhammad ibn al-Hasan ibn Muhammad al-Katib al-Baghdadi, presented by Fakhri al-Barudi (1964).

2 The Egyptian work is the anonymous *Kanz al-Fawai'd wa Tanwi'a al-Mawa'id* presently being edited by David Waines and Manuela Marin; The North African work, also anonymous, was edited by Ambrosio Huici Miranda under the title *Kitab al-Tabikh fi' l-Maghrib wa'l-Andalus*, Madrid (1965).

3 Quoted by H. A. R. Gibb, *Arabic Literature*, Oxford (1963), p. 46.

4 See Michael Freeman, 'Sung', in *Food in Chinese Culture*, edited by K. C. Chang, New Haven (1977), pp. 141–192.

5 See article, 'Baghdad', in *Encyclopaedia of Islam*, New Edition, Leiden (1960), Vol. 1, especially at p. 899.

6 *Koran*, Sura al-A'raf, verse 160.

7 See Andrew M. Watson, 'A medieval green revolution', in *The Islamic Middle East, 700–1900*, edited by A. Udovitch, Princeton (1981), pp. 29–58; also the same author's more detailed study, *Agricultural Innovation in the Early Islamic World*, Cambridge (1983).

8 The data in this and the following paragraph have been extracted from *The Book of Curious and Entertaining Information: The Lata'if al-Ma'arif of Tha'alibi*, translated by C. E. Bosworth, Edinburgh (1968).

9 These are all to be found scattered through the important work of Nasr ibn Sayyar al-Warraq mentioned above, footnote 1.

10 The information on Ibrahim's life is taken from the biographical notices of him in Ahmad ibn Ali al-Khatib al-Baghdadi's *Ta'rikh Baghdad*, Beirut, Vol. 6, pp. 142–148 and the *al- Ta'rikh al-Kabir* of Ali ibn al-Hasan ibn al'Asakir, Damascus, 1330/1911, Part 2, pp. 263–285. The lengthy article by Barbier de Meynard, 'Ibrahim, fils de Mahdi', *Journal Asiatique*, Vol. 13 (1869), pp. 201–342, is still useful. Some diverting tales about Ibrahim are also to be found in Richard Burton's translation of *The Book of the Thousand Nights and One Night*, London (1894) Vol. 4.

11 Interesting insights on the institution of this entertainment form may be found in Jahiz's *The Epistle on Singing Girls*, Edited and translated by A.F.L. Beeston, Warminster (1980).

12 Some of Ibrahim's poetry is preserved in the famous book of songs, the *Kitab al-Aghani* by Abu 'l-Faraj al-Isbahani, Cairo (n.d.), Vol. 10, pp. 95–149; poetry of his sister 'Ulayyah is found in the same volume.

13 For this anecdote see the *Muruj al-Dhahab*, by Ali ibn al-Husayn al-Mas'udi, edited by Barbier de Meynard and Pavet de Courteille, Paris (1861–77), Vol. 6, pp. 349 ff.

14 For example, the recipe *al-Barida*, on page 82.

15 Recipe on page 76.

16 Abu 'l-Hasan Ali ibn Muhammad al-Shabushti, *Kitab al-Diyarat*, Edited by K. 'Awwad, Baghdad (1966).

17 Recipe on page 42.

18 Two, for example, appear in this volume on pages 82 and 84.

19 Two are presented here, on pages 40 and 58.

20 See recipe on page 36.

21 For *Shaljamiya* see recipe on page 34; the *Mutajjan* recipes are on pages 56 and 106.

22 al-Baghdadi, op. cit., p. 9.

23 Maxime Rodinson, 'Recherches sur les documents arabes relatifs a la cuisine', *Revue des Etudes Islamiques*, 17 (1949), at p. 106.

24 An expanded version of this section will be found in the author's forthcoming article, 'al-Matbakh', in the New Edition of the *Encyclopaedia of Islam*.

25 David Waines, 'Bread, cereals and society', *Journal of the Economic and Social History of the Orient*, Vol. 30 (1987), pp. 255–285.

26 C. Anne Wilson, *Food and Drink in Britain*, London (1973), p. 66.

27 Recipe on page 46.

28 Recipe on page 56.

29 Recipes on pages 44 and 54.

30 For more detail and two contemporary recipes see this author's article 'Of Carp and Caliphs' in *Petits Propos Culinaires*, London, No. 10 (1982), pp. 41–47.

31 Recipe on page 42.

32 Recipe on page 36.

33 Recipe on page 50.

34 Recipe on page 96.

35 Recipe on page 108.

36 Recipe on page 112.

37 Recipe on page 72.

38 al-Baghdadi, op. cit. p. 65.

39 Recipe on page 88.

A note on the recipes

The modernized versions of these recipes have been devised to provide portions for four persons of moderate appetite. In planning a traditional medieval meal more than one dish would be served at the table at the same time. Our concept of a meal comprising several distinct courses is alien to this milieu. It would, however, be in keeping with medieval custom to have a side dish of dates with which to commence the meal (see recipes on pages 38 and 104) and end with a fresh fruit salad. With this in mind, a meat and a chicken dish, therefore, would suffice most dining quartets, certainly if accompanied by rice and, say, a green salad made in your own favourite fashion. However, for larger numbers of guests, you may wish to prepare three 'main' dishes, one meat, one chicken and one fish. In the end, only you are familiar with the capacities (and tolerance!) of your own guests.

A second point concerns the ingredient vinegar, much favoured by medieval banqueters. If the recommended amount in a given recipe seems too much for your own taste, then blunt the acidic edge of the vinegar with slightly more sugar, honey, ground almonds, rice or chick peas, that is, with whatever appears as the balancing factor in the particular preparation.

Finally, a word on spices and herbs. Quantities are never given in the originals, so you have to guess. A reasonable guess comes from experiment combined with your own preferences and judgement, much the same way that the medieval cook would have prepared a dish. If you decide a dash more of this and a pinch less of that suits you better, fine. The best result is what pleases *you* best. 'God willing', of course – the formula with which many a recipe so fittingly ends.

The translations of the Arabic recipes contain a number of terms for measures of ingredients. The following are their approximate modern equivalents, although it should be remembered that the values of weights and measures varied from one place to another in the medieval world.

1 ratl = 12 ugiya = 16 ounces = 1 pint
1 ugiya = 10 dirhams
1 dirham = 6 daniq

THE RECIPES

Ibrahimiya

Ingredients

450 g./1 lb. lamb, diced into 2.5-cm./1-inch cubes
225 g./8 oz. minced lean lamb
2 medium onions, finely chopped
250 ml./8 fl. oz. unsweetened red grape juice
100 g./4 oz. ground almonds
4 tablespoons olive oil
2 teaspoons ground coriander
1 teaspoon ground ginger
1 piece cinnamon bark
1 small piece crystallized mastic (optional)
2 tablespoons rosewater
salt and pepper to taste
black grapes and blanched almonds for garnish

1 Place the cubed lamb with half the olive oil in a medium sized heavy casserole and brown the pieces all over.

2 Add the chopped onion, coriander, ginger, cinnamon bark and mastic (optional) and season to taste with salt and pepper; cover the ingredients with water and simmer for 45 minutes.

3 Meanwhile season the minced lamb with a little salt and pepper and form into kabobs the size of unshelled walnuts. Fry these in the rest of the olive oil until browned.

4 Add the grape juice and ground almonds to the casserole and cook for a further 15 minutes. Should the cooking liquid be too tart for your taste, add a teaspoon or two of sugar; this may not be necessary, however, as the almonds will help reduce the tartness somewhat.

5 Add the kabobs to the casserole laying them on the surface of the meat in the sauce. Cook gently for 30 minutes.

6 Arrange the meat on a serving dish placing the kabobs around the edge; garnish the meat with the black grapes and almonds and sprinkle the dish with rosewater.

Ibrahimiya. Taken from the thirteenth century work by al-Baghdadi. This dish is named after Ibrahim b. al-Mahdi as a tribute to his contribution to the gastronomic comforts of leisured urban society. While it is, therefore, not a preparation actually devised by the pioneer of the Abbasid culinary 'new wave', it does reflect a characteristic of Ibrahim's style using grape juice and almonds in the preparation. The appearance of meat in two forms, diced and in cabobs, belongs more in the fashion of the later period.

CUT THE MEAT into medium sized pieces, and place in a casserole with water to cover, salt to taste, and boil until the juices are given off. Throw in a bag of stout cotton containing coriander, ginger, pepper, all ground fine, then add some pieces of cinnamon bark and mastic. Cut up two or three onions very small, and throw in. Mince red meat and make into cabobs as usual, and add. When the ingredients are cooked, remove the bag of seasonings. Add to the broth the juice of sweet old grapes or, if unprocurable, of fresh grapes, squeezing in the hand without skinning, or else distilled vinegar. The juice is strained then sweet almonds are chopped fine and moistened in water, the grape juice is poured on them, and the mixture is sweetened slightly with white sugar, so as not to be too sour. Leave over the fire an hour to settle. Wipe the sides of the casserole with a clean cloth and sprinkle with rose water. When settled, remove.

Shaljamiya

Ingredients

675 g./1½ lb. chicken, half breasts, half
  thighs, cut into 1 cm./½-inch-wide strips
150 g./5 oz. chick peas, soaked one hour in
  water (or 1 tin pre-cooked)
75 g./3 oz. spring onions, chopped
450 g./1 lb. white turnip, or swede
50 g./2 oz. ground almonds
75 g./3 oz. goat's cheese (Feta)
4 egg whites
3 tablespoons olive oil
2½ teaspoons ground cumin
1 tablespoon Dijon mustard
salt and black pepper to taste
fresh coriander or parsley for garnish

1 Set the oven at 200C, 400F or Gas Mark 6.
2 Remove the stalks and peel the
turnip/swede; dice into small pieces and boil
until tender; drain and mash finely or
liquidize.
3 Meanwhile, fry the chicken in the heated
oil, add the onions and chickpeas and
sufficient water to cover. Simmer for 30
minutes.
4 Place the cheese, ground almond and egg
white in the liquidizer and blend to a fine
paste.
5 After the chicken has simmered for 30
minutes add to it pepper, salt, cumin and
mustard. Add the turnip/swede puree and
mix in thoroughly before turning into an
ovenproof dish.
6 Carefully spoon the egg, almond and
cheese paste onto the top of the chicken
mixture and spread evenly over the surface.
7 Bake for 30 minutes. The paste will
become a delicious crust which should be
allowed to brown slightly in the oven.
8 Garnish and serve.

Shaljamiya. This recipe is taken from the earliest extant Arabic culinary
work of al-Warraq. Attributed to Ibrahim b. al-Mahdi, it is one of two in
which he used *shaljam* or turnip, an Arabized word from the Persian
shalgham. Radish is recommended by al-Warraq as a substitute for turnip
in this preparation; or, if turnips were not in season, gourd and onion
could also have been used. In the modernized version here, the vegetable
known in English as swede makes an excellent substitute for turnip, giving
a richer and more distinctive flavour. Ibrahim composed a poem on this
dish in which he compares the turnip to the moon and the stars, or again,
as silver coins.

TAKE THE BREASTS of chicken or other fowl, cut into thin slices and place in a pot with a lot of oil adding water to cover. Remove the scum. Throw in chick peas and olive oil and the white of onion and when cooked, sprinkle on top with pepper and cumin. Next take the turnip and boil it until cooked and then mash it so that no hard bits remain in it. Strain in a sieve and place in the pot. Then take shelled almonds and put in a stone mortar adding to it a piece of cheese and bray very fine. Break over this the whites of five eggs and pound until it becomes very soft. Put this mixture over the turnip and if there is milk in it, put in a bit of nard and leave on the fire to settle. Serve it with mustard.

Badhinjan mahshi

Ingredients
2 large aubergines (about 675 g./1½ lb. in
   weight)
pinch of salt
275 g./10 oz. onions, finely chopped
175 ml./6 fl. oz. white wine vinegar
1½ tablespoons brown sugar
25 g./1 oz. ground almonds
½ teaspoon turmeric
1 teaspoon ground cinnamon
½ teaspoon caraway seeds
1½ tablespoons sesame oil
1–2 tablespoons olive oil (optional)

1 Cut the aubergines into quarters
lengthwise. Place in a pan, cover with
water, add a pinch of salt and simmer for 15
minutes. If the aubergines are too long for
the pan, cut them in half widthwise. Drain
and place the pieces on kitchen towel to soak
up the excess liquid.
2 Meanwhile fry the onions in the sesame oil
until crisp and brown.
3 Place the vinegar, ground almonds, sugar,
turmeric and cinnamon in a liquidizer and
blend. Add the caraway seeds and then pour
the mixture into a shallow serving dish.
4 Arrange the aubergine pieces in the dish
and cover them with the fried onion. (If
desired a tablespoon or so of olive oil could
be sprinkled over the dish at this point.)
Serve cold.

Badhinjan mahshi. This is one of a wide range of dishes known collectively
as *bawarid*, that is, cold dishes. They were made from various vegetables
featuring, for example, carrots, gourd, and beet. Examples of such cold
dishes can also be found made from meat, poultry (see recipe on page 82)
or fish. This particular preparation is attributed also to Ibrahim b. al-
Mahdi who was very fond of the vegetable. Medieval physicians regarded
aubergine as an excellent food specifically because of its property of
causing any obstruction in the kidney or spleen to be removed.

*T*AKE THE AUBERGINE *and stew it. Cut it up into small pieces after stewing. Next take a serving dish and put into it vinegar, white sugar and crushed almonds, saffron, caraway and cinnamon. Then take the aubergine and the fried onion and put them in the dish. Pour oil over it and serve, God willing.*

Rutab mu'assal

Ingredients
450 g./1 lb. fresh dates
2 tablespoons honey
100 g./4 oz. blanched almonds
3 tablespoons rosewater
¼ teaspoon saffron (or turmeric)
2 tablespoons castor sugar
2 tablespoons ground cinnamon

1 Carefully slit each date down one side and remove the stone.
2 Into each date place one blanched almond and squeeze closed.
3 Mix together rosewater, honey and saffron (or turmeric) in a small saucepan, bring to the boil and simmer for three minutes. Remove and allow to cool slightly.
4 Add dates to the syrup, spooning it over the dates so that each is thoroughly coated; leave them in the syrup for a couple of hours.
5 Remove the dates and roll each one in the castor sugar into which the ground cinnamon has been mixed.
6 Serve in paper sweet cases on a plate or tray.

Rutab mu'assal. In English, this literally means 'honeyed dates'. Dates were the common staple food of rural and nomadic populations throughout the Middle East where the hardy date palms of the arid and semi-arid zones produced vast quantities and varieties of this nourishing fruit. The Prophet Muhammad was reported to have said that dates possessed the special quality of dispelling poison and magic. He also is said to have commented that a household without dates was a hungry one. This preparation, from the thirteenth century, has all the features of the more sophisticated urban cooking tradition in its use of rosewater, almonds, musk, camphor and hyacinth. Only the first two need to be used, however, to enjoy this dish.

*T*AKE FRESHLY GATHERED DATES *and lay in the shade and air for a day. Then remove the stones and stuff with peeled almonds. For every ten* ratls *of dates take two* ratls *of honey. Boil over the fire with two* uqiya *of rose water and half a* dirham *of saffron, then throw in the dates, stirring for an hour. Remove and allow to cool. When cold, sprinkle with fine-ground sugar scented with musk, camphor and hyacinth. Put into glass preserving jars, sprinkling on top some of the scented ground sugar. Cover until the weather is cold and chafing dishes are brought in.*

Zirbaj

Ingredients

1 chicken, weight 1.5 kg./3–3½-lb., jointed
50 g./2 oz. spring onions chopped, cut back
   just into the green colour
2 tablespoons olive oil
350 ml./12 fl. oz. white wine vinegar
   (tarragon flavoured optional)
4 tablespoons castor sugar
3 tablespoons rosewater
1½ teaspoons ground cinnamon
¾ teaspoon ground ginger
25 g./1 oz. ground almonds
25 g./1 oz. flaked almonds
pepper to taste
chopped parsley for garnish

1 Heat the oil in a large casserole, place the chicken pieces into it and brown lightly on all sides.
2 Add the chopped onions and pepper to taste, cover the chicken with water, bring to the boil and simmer for half an hour.
3 Combine together in a bowl the vinegar, rosewater, sugar, cinnamon, ginger and almonds, stir briefly and add mixture to the chicken. Simmer a further half hour.
4 Turn out the chicken into a shallow serving dish and garnish with chopped parsley.

Zirbaj. There are many varieties of this dish which is of Persian origin. The tenth century compiler of recipes, al-Warraq, includes this in a chapter of his work entitled *zirbaj* preparations and those, such as the one given here, made *a la* Ibrahim b. al-Mahdi. The sweet and sour flavours (in this case provided by the sugar and vinegar) were a common feature of dishes of Persian origin and may be found today in certain North African preparations.

*T*AKE A FINE *quality chicken, joint it and clean it and place it in a clean pot. Then pour over one half* ratl *of fresh water and one half* uqiya *of a good quality oil, some white of onion and boil together. When boiled, pour in white vinegar, a half* ratl *and two* uqiya *of white sugar and one* uqiya *peeled almonds, and one* uqiya *of rose water. Add spices, pepper, cinnamon and ginger tied up in a fine cloth so that they do not alter the dish's colour. Place on the fire a little allowing it to thicken.*

Sibagh

Ingredients
450 g./1 lb. smoked cod or haddock
100 g./4 oz. seedless raisins
250 ml./8 fl. oz. white wine vinegar
1 clove garlic, crushed
1 teaspoon coriander seeds, crushed
olive oil
parsley and lemon wedges for garnish

1 Soak the raisins and the garlic in the vinegar for at least one hour beforehand and then liquidize the mixture. If the mixture is too tart for your taste add a spoonful of sugar and blend in.
2 Heat the oil in a frying pan and add the crushed coriander seeds. Fry the fish three or four minutes on both sides.
3 Pour the sauce onto a serving plate and place the fish on top taking care not to allow it to break into pieces. Garnish with parsley and wedges of lemon.

Sibagh. This is a general term for many kinds of seasoning or condiment and applies here specifically to the sauce to accompany fish. The preparation is attributed to Ibrahim b. al-Mahdi. Recipes have also come down to us for poultry dishes. One type of *sibagh* was used by travellers and came for convenience in the shape of small dried cakes made of currants and pomegranate seeds which, when ready for use, could be reconstituted with vinegar. The purpose of such condiments at meals was to cleanse the palate of the oiliness of certain dishes, to stimulate the appetite and assist digestion.

TAKE A HANDFUL of choice raisins and soak them in vinegar. Then mash. Add a little garlic and beat in with the vinegar. Prepare a saucer of this (for serving).

Masliya

Ingredients

450 g./1 lb. fillet end of lamb, cut into
   3.5-cm/1½-inch lengths
1 large onion, finely chopped
3 tablespoons olive or sesame oil
225 g./8 oz. fresh spinach, cooked for three
   minutes and coarsely chopped
75 g./3 oz. Gruyère cheese, finely grated
2.5 cm./1 inch piece root ginger, peeled and
   cut in two
1 small cinnamon stick
25 g./1 oz. fresh coriander, coarsely chopped
1½ teaspoons coriander seeds, finely ground
1½ teaspoons ground cumin
salt and freshly ground black pepper to taste

1 In the heated oil seal the meat, then add
the onion, ginger and cinnamon. Cover with
water and add the fresh coriander leaves and
a pinch of salt. Simmer for 30 minutes.
2. Add the ground coriander, ground cumin
and pepper. Cook for a further 10 minutes.
3 Add the pre-cooked spinach and cook a
further 10 minutes. Place in a serving dish
and sprinkle over the grated cheese.

Masliya. This preparation, also one by Ibrahim b. al-Mahdi, has a distinct
Arab character about it. *Masl*, a by-product of milk, is variously described
as dried curds, cooked and dried whey, or dried milk. In any event, milk
was part of the staple diet of the Beduin and was considered by them to be
'one of the two meats' (the other, of course, being meat flesh). In its dried
form it could be kept for a long while until needed when it required being
chopped into small pieces for the cooking pot. Galingal (*khulinjan* in
Persian) of the greater variety belongs to the ginger family and the two are
often found together in medieval dishes. Like ginger, it is the spicy root of
the plant which is used, and as galingal is difficult to obtain ginger alone
makes a good substitute. For convenience, spinach has been substituted
for beet leaves in modernized version of the recipe.

*T*AKE THE MEAT *of a small young animal and cut it into finger like strips and place it in the pot after cleaning it thoroughly. Pour over it fine oil, a stick each of galingal and cinnamon and add fresh coriander and chopped onion. Cook and when nearly done, sprinkle over it pepper, dried coriander and ground cumin. Next boil beet (leaves) and add to the pot. Then chop up* masl *very fine and place over the contents and present it. God willing.*

Isfanakhiya

Ingredients

450 g./1 lb. fillet end of leg of lamb (half
    minced and half cut into 2.5-cm./1-inch
    cubes)
50 g./2 oz. chick-peas, soaked in hot water
    for one hour
450 g./1 lb. fresh spinach, chopped or
    225 g./8 oz. frozen leaf spinach
25 g./1 oz. long grain rice
25 g./1 oz. butter
a little olive oil
4 teaspoons ground coriander
2 teaspoons ground cumin
1 teaspoon ground cinnamon
1 piece cinnamon bark
2 cloves crushed garlic
½ teaspoon salt
1 teaspoon ground allspice
freshly ground black pepper to taste

1 Place the cubed meat in a heavy casserole
and fry it in the butter to seal in the juices.
Cover with water, add salt and boil for 20
minutes. Remove any scum.
2 Add chick-peas and chopped washed
spinach, then add 3 teaspoons of the
coriander, cumin, garlic, cinnamon bark and
pepper. Add more water if necessary and
simmer for half an hour.
3 Add the rice and simmer for a further 15
minutes or until the rice is cooked, again
adding water if necessary.
4 Meanwhile take the minced lamb, add the
other teaspoon of coriander, allspice and a
pinch of salt and mix thoroughly. Form the
meat into walnut-sized cabobs and fry in the
oil until brown all over.
5 Place the cabobs on the surface of the
cooking contents of the casserole and
simmer 15 minutes.
6 Arrange in a serving dish placing the
cabobs on top; sprinkle with ground
cinnamon and serve hot.

Isfanakhiya. Many dishes of the medieval cuisine were designated by their
most characteristic ingredient, here the vegetable spinach (*isfanakh* from
the Greek) even though it is prepared with meat. 'Tail' (*alya*) refers here to
the fatty tail of the sheep which was perhaps the most commonly
employed medium for browning meat. Mastic, a resinous substance, is
drawn from a bush found widespread in the hilly regions around the
Mediterranean. The hard crystals can be chewed like gum or used to
flavour cooked dishes. This particular preparation is somewhat unusual as
rice is used as the thickening agent rather than ground almonds, chick-
peas, or breadcrumbs.

*T*AKE FAT MEAT *and cut into medium-sized pieces. Slice the fresh tail, dissolve, and remove the sediment. Put the meat into this oil and stir until browned. Then cover with water that has been heated separately. Add a little salt, boil and remove the scum. Throw in a handful of chick-peas that have been soaked and peeled. Take fresh spinach, wash, remove the lower roots, and cut with a knife into finger-lengths, then pound in a stone mortar, and put into the saucepan. When nearly cooked, add dry coriander, cumin, brayed pepper, mastic, small pieces of cinnamon bark and a little garlic crushed fine. Now fill with water as required, letting the water be lukewarm. When it has boiled awhile, add clean washed rice as required, placing it over the fire until it is set firm and smooth. Then leave over a slow flame for an hour and remove. Meanwhile prepare red meat minced fine and made into cabobs and fry these in oil with the usual seasonings. When the concoction is ladled out, strew over it this fried meat, together with the oil as required, sprinkle with fine-ground cinnamon and serve.*

Rukhamiya

Ingredients
450 g./1 lb. minced leg of lamb
100 g./4 oz. long grain rice, soaked for an
    hour in 250 ml./8 fl. oz. of milk
2 tablespoons olive oil
1 teaspoon ground coriander
1 teaspoon ground cumin
1 teaspoon ground cinnamon
½ teaspoon salt
freshly ground black pepper to taste

1 Season the minced lamb with coriander
and *half* the ground cumin and cinnamon;
add salt and pepper to taste and form into
cabobs about the size of walnuts. Fry in oil
until browned all over. Set aside and keep
warm.
2 Meanwhile cook the rice in the milk in
which it has been soaking, adding the rest of
the cinnamon and cumin. Adjust seasoning
with salt. Cook slowly over a low heat until
the mixture thickens.
3 Place the rice in a serving dish and
arrange the cabobs on top. Sprinkle with a
little ground cumin.

Rukhamiya. This is from the thirteenth century work of al-Baghdadi. The
name of the dish comes from the Arabic meaning 'marble' (*rukham*) and is
possibly suggested by the contrasting colours of the rice cooked in milk
and the fried meat which in another variation is sprinkled over the rice in
minced form together with cinnamon. It is one of the few 'rice dishes' to be
found in the medieval repertoire, another being the 'peppered rice' in the
recipe on page 98.

COOK RICE *with milk until set thick, then ladle out. Place on top of this meat fried in tail fat and seasonings in the form of cabobs as in the preceding recipe. Sprinkle with cinnamon.*

Mishmishiya

Ingredients
675 g./1½ lb. lamb, cubed
1 large onion, finely sliced
3 tablespoons olive oil
175 g./6 oz. dried apricots, soaked in hot
　　water one hour
50 g./2 oz. ground almonds
rosewater
¼ teaspoon turmeric
½ teaspoon ground coriander
½ teaspoon ground cumin
¼ teaspoon ground cinnamon
¼ teaspoon ground ginger
freshly ground black pepper to taste
salt to taste

1 Heat the oil in a heavy casserole and brown the pieces of meat on all sides.
2 Stir in the spices and season to taste with salt and pepper and cook a further 5 minutes.
3 Add the onion and the water in which the apricots were soaked and enough additional water to cover the meat. Bring to the boil and lower the heat then simmer for an hour or until the meat is tender.
4 Stir in the ground almonds and add the apricots and continue cooking until the fruit is soft but not disintegrating.
5 Turn into a serving dish and sprinkle with rosewater.

Mishmishiya. The apricot (*mishmish*) was also known in Arabic as the Armenian apple (*tuffah armani*). A dish such as this, from the thirteenth century cookbook by al-Baghdadi, could have been assembled from ingredients purchased in the major markets of Baghdad which had been brought from regions in the Abbasid domains specialized in certain food products. For example, Tus in northeast Persia was famous for its apricots; saffron was a speciality of Isfahan; and the finest rosewater, obtained from the province of Fars, was known as Juri. Some 30,000 flasks of Juri were sent to the Caliphs in Baghdad each year along with the provincial land tax.

CUT FAT MEAT SMALL, put into the saucepan with a little salt and cover with water. Boil and remove the scum. Cut up onions, wash and throw in on top of the meat. Add seasonings, coriander, cumin, mastic, cinnamon, pepper, and ginger, all well-ground. Take dry apricots, soak in hot water, then wash and put into a separate saucepan and boil lightly. Take out and wipe in the hands and strain through a sieve. Take the juice and add it to the saucepan to form a broth. Take sweet almonds, grind fine, moisten with a little apricot juice and throw in. Some colour it with a little saffron. Spray the saucepan with a little rose water, wipe its sides with a clean rag and leave to settle over the fire. Then remove.

Baid Masus

Ingredients

25 g./1 oz. celery leaves with their stocks,
   chopped fine

½ tablespoon sesame oil

a few strands of saffron or ¼ teaspoon
   turmeric

50 ml./2 fl oz. cider vinegar

½ teaspoon coriander seeds, roasted and
   crushed

½ teaspoon caraway seeds roasted and
   crushed

¼ teaspoon ground cinnamon

2 eggs

salt to taste

1 Put the oil in a frying pan, add and stir the celery leaves, around in the pan.

2 Roast together the coriander and caraway seeds and then pound in a mortar along with the cinnamon. Add to the frying pan, stir in, and heat the ingredients gently for about three minutes. Then add the cider vinegar with saffron (or turmeric) and cook for another couple of minutes.

3 Beat the eggs lightly, season with salt, then pour into a heated pan and stir the mixture gently until it sets.

Baid Masus. Dishes called *masus* were commonly made from meat and poultry, their characteristic feature being vinegar, which was absorbed or 'sucked up' (from the verb *massa*) by the other ingredients during the cooking. This is one of many egg preparations in the medieval corpus of recipes and comes from an anonymous work probably of Egyptian origin. The same recipe appears in the thirteenth century recipe collection of al-Baghdadi.

*P*UT SOME SESAME OIL *in a frying pan. Celery leaves (removed) from their stalks are then chopped up and added to the oil and fried. Then, sprinkling over this sufficient amounts of cinnamon, mastic, coriander, caraway, next pour some vinegar into the mixture, as much as required, colouring with a little saffron. When the mixture has been heated, adjust with salt, then break the egg and add to it. Cover the pan until the (egg) is cooked and serve.*

Madira

Ingredients

450 g./1 lb. lean lamb, cut into thin slices
350 ml./12 fl. oz. goat's or sheep's yoghurt
1 large aubergine, about 450 g./16 oz.
1 Indian gourd
1 onion
juice of 1 lemon
225 g./8 oz. fresh or tinned asparagus
  (optional)
1 bunch fresh mint (4–5 sprigs tied together)
1½ teaspoons dried mint
3 teaspoons ground coriander
1½ teaspoons ground cumin
salt

1 Add half the lemon juice to the yoghurt.
2 Cut the aubergine into cubes; peel and cut the gourd into cubes. Slice the onion. Place them all in a bowl, sprinkle with the remaining lemon juice and a level tablespoon of salt and allow to stand for an hour.
3 Place the meat in a saucepan and add just sufficient water to cover, together with a pinch of salt. Simmer for 20 minutes, uncovered, and then add the yoghurt to the reduced liquid and simmer for 10 more minutes. Remove from the heat.
4 When the vegetables are ready, place them in a colander and wash off the excess salt. Then add the vegetables to the meat, together with the bunch of fresh mint, dried mint, coriander and cumin and cook for a further 30 minutes. Remove the bunch of fresh mint.
5 If you decide to use fresh asparagus, trim and use the top 10–13 cm./4–5 inches adding them to the pot, simmering gently in a covered pan until they are tender. If using tinned asparagus, add and warm them through.
6 Turn out onto a serving dish and arrange the asparagus and some more sprigs of mint around the plate as garnish.

Madira. One of the classic Arab dishes, so-called because it is cooked with sour milk, which 'bites the tongue'. In order to get the proper degree of bite, fresh milk would be mixed with milk gathered in a goat's skin bag which would quickly sour it. Its original, rustic preparation was simplicity itself. Here, in the hands of Ibrahim b. al-Mahdi, a transformation has occurred to suit the urban palate, Ibrahim using his favourite vegetable the aubergine. The dish was judged to be so tempting that people could be driven to renounce their fast in order to indulge in it. Also deemed comforting for whatever ailment afflicted you, the dish was called 'the miracle food'.

*T*AKE MILK in sufficient amount for the meat and let it be of moderate sourness; if it is too sour, then let (the proportion) be two thirds sour milk and one third fresh milk. Light a gentle fire under it and set (the pot) on it covered, and be patient for an hour so that the sour milk settles to the bottom and the water rises to the top. Strain the water from it and set aside. Next take the meat from the shoulder (of the animal) and the ribs next to it, cut up into thin slices and wash. Stew lightly if you are in a hurry. Then remove from the pot and cover with cold water, allowing it to be absorbed. When the water has been drawn off from it, the pot with the sour milk is placed on the fire after the meat has been added to it. Kindle a gentle fire under it so that when the (contents) have boiled twice, you then peel and chop aubergine and gourd and onion round and place in water and salt for an hour. Add to the pot so that when it boils again, a bunch of mint is then added. When the contents have thickened, the water previously strained (from the sour milk) is sprinkled over it little by little. Wipe around the pot and leave it on the embers. Do not add any spices except cumin alone. Then remove the bunch of mint and add fresh mint so that it does not become blackened; if this, however, is not a matter of concern, then add dried coriander to the cumin. And, if asparagus is plentiful, use some.

Mutajjan bi sadr al-dajjaj

Ingredients
450 g./1 lb. chicken breasts, cut into strips
   2.5-cm./1-inch wide
2 tablespoons olive oil
15 g./$\frac{1}{2}$ oz. coarsely chopped fresh coriander
250 ml./8 fl. oz. white wine vinegar
25 g./1 oz. coarsely ground almond halves,
   roasted
$\frac{1}{2}$ teaspoon sumac
$\frac{1}{4}$ teaspoon ground black pepper
salt to taste
black olives for garnish

1 Heat the oil in a heavy based pan and fry the chicken evenly on all sides. When cooked through add the coriander, pepper, sumac and salt, stirring for 2 or 3 minutes.
2 Add the vinegar and cook gently for 5 minutes more.
3 Put into a serving dish and sprinkle the almonds on top, garnishing with as many olives as desired.

Mutajjan bi-sadr al-dajjaj. A simple dish of Ibrahim's which simply means pieces of chicken breast (*sadr al-dajjaj*) fried in a *tajin*. The ingredient *murri* is a prepared condiment or seasoning which is impossible to replicate in the modern home, as it requires many weeks of labour intensive preparation commencing in the spring and lasting throughout the height of the summer heat. To say that it is made from barley flour seasoned with a variety of spices conveys no impression of its complexity. One recipe suggests as a substitute the spice sumac; as its rather astringent citrus-like flavour works well in dishes where it is ordinarily used, this substitution has been made throughout these recipes. *Murri* is said to have warming properties causing thirst and dryness in the body, in which respect it is even stronger than salt. This effect of *murri* can be countered by either drinking water or eating something sweet.

*T*AKE CHICKEN BREASTS *sliced, cut up into small pieces and fry in oil until they appear to be cooked. Add to them pepper, fresh coriander and sprinkle over them vinegar and* murri *and then spread ground almonds on top. God willing.*

Zirbajat al-Safarjal

Ingredients
1 chicken (about 1.5 kg./3–3½ lb. in weight) jointed into 6 pieces and skin removed
100 g./4 oz. tinned chick-peas
450 g./1 lb. small to medium onions, peeled
250 ml./8 fl. oz. white wine vinegar
3 tablespoons olive oil
675 g./1½ lb. quinces, peeled, quartered and cored
100 g./4 oz. wholemeal (or golden) breadcrumbs
2.5 cm./1 inch piece of root ginger, peeled and cut in two
3 teaspoons coriander seeds, roasted and ground together with
3 teaspoons cumin powder
salt and pepper to taste
fresh coriander or red pepper for garnish

1 Place the chicken pieces in a pan with the ginger, whole onions, salt to taste and oil. Just cover with water and simmer for 30 minutes with the pan partly covered. At the end remove the onions and discard them.
2 Meanwhile gently stew the quinces in about 600 ml./1 pint of water in another pan for at least 20 minutes so that the quinces have fallen apart. Strain the juice and reserve, discarding the quince pulp.
3 Next add to the chicken, the vinegar, the chick-peas, the quince juice, the coriander, cumin and pepper to taste, cover the pan and cook over a low heat for another 30 minutes. About 15 minutes before the end of the cooking time, add the breadcrumbs and stir them in well. Turn out into a serving dish and garnish with fresh coriander or diced red pepper.

Zirbajat al-Safarjal. This is another variety of *zirbaj* as found in the recipe of that name (page 40). It is also one of Ibrahim's. The ingredient featured in it is quince (*safarjal*) juice, which together with the vinegar, gives the dish a pleasantly tart flavour. According to medieval medical lore, *zirbaj* dishes in general were unsuited for persons with 'weak stomachs'. Quince, however, is recommended as a counterbalancing ingredient for *zirbaj*, so this dish ought to suit everyone's stomach.

*T*AKE ONE YOUNG *plump chicken, joint it and place it in a clean pot. Put with it a stick of galingal, a handful of soaked and peeled chickpeas and a ratl of whole onions and a little salt. Pour over this sufficient water and salt to cover (the contents of the pot) and one third uqiya of oil. Then place the pot on the fire until the onion is cooked; then remove all the onion so that none is left and then discard. Next, pour into the pot a quarter ratl of vinegar and wait until it has cooked. Then pour into (the pot) a ratl of fresh quince juice which has been pressed that day and add half an uqiya dried coriander and half a dirhem pepper and likewise half of nard, three dirhems of cumin and twenty dirhems of the choice pith of bread. Remove from the fire, wash around the pot and leave to settle. Then present (at table) God willing.*

Isfidhbaja Khadra

Ingredients
450 g./1 lb. fillet of lamb, cut into
   2.5-cm./1-inch cubes
100 g./4 oz. chopped onions
3 tablespoons olive oil
50 g./2 oz. goat's milk cheese (feta)
1 head celery, coarsely chopped
25 g./1 oz. fresh coriander
3 tablespoons ground coriander
1 stick cinnamon
$\frac{1}{2}$ teaspoon ground cinnamon
1 level teaspoon black pepper
salt to taste

1 Heat the oil and brown the meat on all sides. Add the onions and cinnamon stick and cover with water allowing it to simmer for 30 minutes.
2 Meanwhile boil the chopped celery and fresh coriander in 900 ml./1$\frac{1}{2}$ pints of water. When the celery is tender, place the contents in a blender and liquidize. Pour through a sieve and retain the liquor as stock for the meat.
3 Add the stock to the meat, then the cheese, crumbled, the dried coriander, pepper, ground cinnamon and salt to taste.
4 Cook over a moderate heat for a further hour until the liquid is much reduced, skimming off the fat if necessary. Turn into a serving dish and garnish with fresh coriander.

Isfidhbaja Khadra. The famous tenth century physician, al-Razi, says of this variety of dish that it is very healthy, being suitable for most conditions and occasions, for all ages and for all persons of voracious temperament, except the truly gluttonous. Those, however, inclined towards a temperament governed by yellow bile would find this dish unsuitable on its own; they would be advised to eat it with some kind of sour tasting fruit followed by a helping of *sikbaj* (see recipe on page 76). The *kanun* is a clay or mud brick hearth used for cooking. In this recipe, Ibrahim has employed a common practice of making a kind of quick vegetable stock in which to flavour the dish at a secondary stage of the preparation; here it is made of celery and fresh coriander water.

*T*AKE SOME FOUR ratls *of meat, cut it up bit by bit and place in a pot with a piece of cinnamon, a ratl of onion chopped up and a third of a ratl of oil with some salt as required. Cover with water and then place the pot quickly on a portable stove or a* kanun. *When the contents are half cooked, throw in with it pieces of cheese to the amount of five* dirhems. *When almost completely cooked, add a total of half a ratl of the water of coriander and celery, then pound dried coriander and a* dirhem *of pepper and half a* dirhem *of cinnamon. Leave until the contents have settled. Remove and serve. God willing.*

Khashkhashiya

Ingredients
450 g./1 lb. lamb shoulder or leg, sliced into
   strips
2 tablespoons olive oil
2 tablespoons honey
75 g./3 oz. white poppy seeds, lightly roasted
1 tablespoon ground coriander
1 teaspoon ground cinnamon
1 teaspoon ground ginger
a few strands of saffron or $\frac{1}{2}$ teaspoon
   turmeric
3 tablespoons rosewater
salt to taste

1 Heat the oil in a pan and fry the meat until browned all over. Then add the ground coriander, cinnamon, ginger and a pinch of salt to the pan and coat the meat thoroughly in these seasonings. Cover the meat with water and simmer gently for 45 minutes, adding a little water if necessary.
2 Meanwhile add the honey, saffron or turmeric to 300 ml./$\frac{1}{2}$ pint of boiling water and stir until the honey has dissolved. Then put the poppy seeds in a frying pan and lightly roast them, allowing them to crackle for about 5 minutes, taking care to keep stirring so they won't burn. Add them to the water and honey and mix in well.
3 Add the poppy seed sauce to the meat and simmer for a further half hour allowing the sauce to become reduced.
4 Sprinkle the rosewater over the contents of the pan, leave for another minute and then serve.

Khashkhashiya. This thirteenth century recipe from al-Baghdadi's work takes its name from the poppy seed flour (*samidh khashkhashi*) used to thicken the stock. While many kinds of poppy are used for ornamental purposes, it is the opium poppy, also of many varieties, that is important in the culinary sense. The modernized version calls for the Indian type of seed which is off-white, but the Western type which is slate blue in colour can be used equally well. As the seeds are hard to grind they should be first lightly roasted before crushing; this also releases a nutty, sweet-spicy aroma from the seeds which strengthens their flavour.

*C*UT RED MEAT *into small slices. Melt fresh tail fat and throw in the meat to fry lightly. Drop in half a* dirhem, *and the same quantity of brayed dry coriander. Then cover with tepid water, boil and skim. Then add fine chopped cinnamon bark, and a little fine-ground ginger. Make a broth with one and a half* ratl *of hot water, and add one hundred and fifty* dirhems *of sugar or honey. When the sugar is dissolved, sprinkle in a handful of poppy flour. Stir well until cooked and set. Then throw in thirty* dirhems *of fresh poppy. Or, if this is not attainable, dry poppy soaked and ground. Stir until well mixed. Colour with saffron and spray over the top a little rose water. Wipe the sides of the pot with a clean rag and leave to settle over a slow fire for an hour; then remove.*

Malih bi-laban

Ingredients
450 g./1 lb. cod or haddock fillet
2 tablespoons sesame or olive oil
475 ml./16 fl. oz. natural yoghurt
2 cloves garlic, crushed
1 teaspoon ground cinnamon
3 teaspoons ground cumin
2 teaspoons coriander seeds, roasted and
　ground
1 teaspoon ground coriander
1 teaspoon salt
parsley, red or green pepper for garnish

1 Rub the salt into the fish and leave to stand an hour; then wash the fish, dry on a kitchen towel and cut into strips about 3.5 cm./$1\frac{1}{2}$ inches wide.
2 Heat the oil, add the coriander seeds and fry the fish.
3 Chop the garlic finely and mix, with the remaining spices, thoroughly into the yoghurt.
4 Place the cooked fish on a serving dish and pour over it the yoghurt sauce. Garnish with parsley or red and green pepper. Serve immediately or eat as a cold dish.

Malih bi-laban. In some parts of the modern Arab world there is a deep suspicion that fish and milk are in some manner a poisonous combination and thus should be avoided. This recipe from al-Baghdadi has worked very well in practice and to the best of this writer's knowledge, no fatalities (or even upset stomachs) have been recorded as a result of its ingestion.

*T*AKE SALTED FISH, *wash and clean and then fry in sesame oil. Take out while hot, and drop into milk in which garlic has been placed. Sprinkle with fine-ground cumin, coriander and cinnamon. Eat either hot or cold.*

Samak mishwa

Ingredients
6 thick cod or haddock steaks
50 g./2 oz. walnuts, finely chopped
2 teaspoons sumac
2 cloves garlic, crushed
1 teaspoon dried thyme
1 teaspoon coriander seeds, crushed in a
   mortar
1 teaspoon cumin
½ teaspoon cinnamon
2 tablespoons rosewater
2 tablespoons sesame oil
a few strands of saffron
salt to taste

1 Preheat the oven to 180C, 350F or Gas Mark 4.
2 Mix together the sumac, thyme, garlic, cumin, coriander, cinnamon, walnuts and salt. Add one tablespoon of sesame oil and mix to a paste.
3 In a small glass allow the strands of saffron to 'bleed' into the rosewater a few minutes; then add the other tablespoon of sesame oil. With this mixture brush the fish steaks all over as well as the bottom of a shallow baking dish.
4 Stuff each steak with the walnut mixture and place in the baking dish. Bake in the oven for 30 minutes. After 15 minutes brush the steaks again with the oil and rosewater mixture.
5 Sprinkle the steaks with cinnamon and cumin. Serve hot or cold.

Samak mishwa. Al-Razi, taking his cue from the Greek physician Galen described fish in general to be bad and difficult to digest. Although al-Razi was himself knowledgeable in matters of the kitchen, his professional medical opinion did not accord with that of contemporary gourmands who delighted in dishes such as this one.

*T*AKE FRESH FISH, and scrape off the skin very well with a knife. Split open, wash thoroughly and dry. Take sumac, grind fine and discard the seeds. Take half of this quantity of dry thyme and also grind, together with a quarter as much garlic, skinned and chopped fine. Now take half the total quantity of walnuts and chop and mix all together, adding a little fine ground coriander, cumin, cinnamon and mastic. Make this into a paste with fresh sesame oil, adding salt to taste. Smear the fish with sesame oil and saffron mixed with rose water inside and out. Then stuff with the stuffing described. Tie up with strong cotton threads and place on an iron skewer. Place in the oven over a gentle fire, not blazing. Cover and leave to cook well, then remove. This can be eaten hot or cold.

Khushknanaj

Ingredients
175 g./6 oz. strong white flour
15 g./½ oz. yeast
50 g./2 oz. ground almonds
50 g./2 oz. castor sugar
1 teaspoon ground coriander
1 teaspoon ground cinnamon
1 tablespoon olive oil
2–3 tablespoons rosewater
3 tablespoons milk
1 teaspoon granulated sugar
40 g./1½ oz. granulated sugar
15 g./½ oz. chopped almonds
pinch of salt

1 Sieve the flour into a bowl and add a pinch of salt.
2 Cream the yeast with one teaspoon of granulated sugar and a little water and add to the flour. Add the tablespoon of olive oil. Next add sufficient tepid water so as to mix the dough to a firm consistency, and knead on a floured board for 10 minutes. Cover the bowl and leave in a warm place to prove for an hour and a half.
3 Meanwhile make the stuffing. Mix together the ground almonds, the castor sugar, the coriander and the cinnamon. When all these ingredients are thoroughly blended bind the mixture into a stiff paste by gradually adding to it the rosewater.
4 When the dough has risen turn it out onto a floured board and knead for a couple of minutes. Next cut the dough into ten equal portions and roll each into a flat, thin, oval shape. Then take a tenth of the stuffing mixture and shape it into a cigarette roll about 2.5 cm./1 inch shorter than the length of the oval dough pieces. Place the stuffing on the dough, wet the edges with water, then draw them together over the stuffing and shape into cylindrical rolls. Be careful to seal the stuffing well inside so it will not spill out during the baking.
5 Place the rolls on a greased baking tin and cook in a hot oven (230C, 450F or Gas Mark 8) until browned.
6 While the rolls are baking make a glaze by melting the 40 g./1½ oz. of granulated sugar in 3 tablespoons of milk in a pot over low heat. When the sugar has melted remove from the heat and add a tablespoon of rosewater. When the rolls are cooked, remove from the oven and brush with the glaze; then sprinkle a little chopped almond on each roll.

Khushknanaj. This thirteenth century preparation from al-Baghdadi's manual belongs to a section of sweetmeats which include the recipes for *Hais* (recipe on page 104) and *Rutab mu'assal* (recipe on page 38). The word itself is derived from the Persian, *khushk* meaning 'dry' and *nan* meaning bread.

*T*AKE FINE WHITE FLOUR *and with every* ratl *mix three* uqiya *of sesame oil, kneading into a firm paste. Leave to rise. Then make into long loaves. Put into the middle of each loaf a suitable quantity of ground almonds and scented sugar mixed with rose water, using half as much almonds as sugar. Then press together as usual and bake in the oven. Remove.*

Sughdiya

Ingredients

450 g./1 lb. lean lamb, minced
450 g./1 lb. lamb shoulder, cut into cubes
225 g./8 oz. chicken breasts, sliced
100 g./4 oz. chick-peas, soaked overnight
2 medium onions, finely chopped
100 g./4 oz. ground almonds
50 g./2 oz. fresh coriander, chopped fine
2 eggs, yolks and whites separated
1 tablespoon sesame seed oil
2 tablespoons olive oil
2 teaspoons dried dill weed
1 teaspoon ground cinnamon
2 teaspoons ground coriander
1 teaspoon ground cumin
salt to taste

1 Place the cubed lamb in a casserole with the onion, sesame seed oil, fresh coriander, cinnamon and salt to taste. Cover with water and simmer for 30 minutes, removing any scum that may form on the surface.
2 Add the chicken, chick-peas and dill weed and cook for a further 30 minutes, adding water if necessary.
3 Meanwhile, season the minced lamb with the ground coriander and cumin, adding a pinch of salt and form the meat into small cabobs. Heat the olive oil in a frying pan and fry the cabobs until browned all over. Reserve and keep warm.
4 Mix the ground almonds with two tablespoons of water; then add the whites of two eggs and stir into a smooth paste. At the end of step two above, add this paste gradually to the cooking contents of the pot, stirring it in thoroughly.
5 Beat the egg yolks and pour on top of the cooking contents of the pot. Then carefully place the cabobs on the surface. Cover the pot and simmer gently for 20 minutes or so. Sprinkle with a little ground cinnamon and cumin and serve.

Sughdiya. Exceptionally, this dish is named after a place rather than an ingredient. Sughd was a district of Persia located between Bukhara and Samarqand in what is now the Soviet Union. The dish, and others like it, were the contributions to the emerging 'haute cuisine' in Baghdad, brought there by individuals from all corners of the empire of the Abbasid dynasty attracted to their cosmopolitan, imperial capital. The original recipe which is quite complicated has been simplified for the modern kitchen.

*C*UT UP FAT MEAT *and throw in the pot with some pieces of onion, two* dirhems *of coriander and scraped cinnamon bark and two* dirhems *of salt. Keep stirring. When juicy and fragrant with the seasonings, throw in a handful of peeled chick peas and stir. If desired, add a cock or chicks quartered. Cover with water. Add a little sesame oil and a little washed dill. When boiling, remove the dill. Take some almonds, peel, grind fine and mix with water. Add to this the white of egg, beat up well; then throw into the pan with salt to taste. Now take thin slices of meat that have been half boiled and flavoured with salt. Lay sticks on top of the pot and place these slices over the sticks to smoke in the ascending vapours. When (the contents) of the pot are cooked, throw the slices of meat on top together with the yolks of egg. Then take red meat, cut up fine with a large knife, and pound in the mortar with seasonings and salt to taste, making into cabobs. Stew with the slices of meat, then remove, and dip them in the whites of the egg; let them be hot so as to absorb the whites and be covered with them. Then put them back into the pot with the slices. Wipe the sides of the pot with a clean cloth, cover, and leave over the fire an hour to settle. Then sprinkle with fine ground cumin and cinnamon, and remove.*

Na'na Mukhallal

100 g./4 oz. fresh mint, coarsely chopped
25 g./1 oz. chopped celery leaves
2 garlic cloves, finely chopped
250 ml./8 fl. oz. wine vinegar
1 teaspoon thyme
1 teaspoon basil
a few strands of saffron

1 Place the mint and all the other ingredients in a tight-lidded bottle or jar. Leave for two to four days until the mint has absorbed the sourness of the vinegar.

Na'na Mukhallal. A medieval mint sauce. Large quantities of such pickles (*mukhallalat*) made from a variety of vegetables (aubergine and turnip were common) were made in the home and stored for daily use over several months. The method used in this thirteenth century recipe is simplicity itself; any moisture in the mint leaves or celery acts effectively to dilute the acid sharpness of the vinegar (*khall*). Pickles served a similar purpose as *sibagh* (recipe on page 42) in aiding digestion. A small plate or bowl of this can be placed on the table alongside the other dishes of the meal and dipped into between mouthfuls.

TAKE FRESH, large leafed mint and strip the leaf from the stalk. Wash and dry in the shade. Sprinkle with aromatic herbs. If desired, add celery leaves and quarters of peeled garlic. Put into a glass bottle and cover with good vinegar, coloured with a little saffron. Leave until the mint has absorbed the sourness of the vinegar so that the latter has lost its sharpness. Then serve.

Tirrikh mufarraka

Ingredients

450 g./1 lb. fillet of cod, haddock or hake,
  cut into small pieces.
2 eggs
3 tablespoons sesame or olive oil
1 tablespoon lemon juice
2 teaspoons ground coriander (or seeds,
  roasted and crushed
1 teaspoon ground cumin (or seeds, roasted
  and crushed)
$\frac{1}{2}$ teaspoon ground cinnamon
pinch of salt
lemon wedges and parsley for garnish

1 Heat the oil and fry the fish with the ground (or crushed) coriander, cumin, cinnamon and salt over a medium heat.
2 Meanwhile beat the eggs.
3 When the fish is cooked, add the lemon juice, stir and then pour the eggs over it, stirring continuously until both the fish and eggs are golden brown.
4 Place in a serving dish and garnish with lemon and parsley.

Tirrikh mufarraka. A recipe from al-Baghdadi's thirteenth century manual. *Tirrikh* (derived from the Greek) was the name of a fish caught in Lake Van in Armenia. The dish for *mufarraka* mentioned in this recipe refers to one for chicken livers, a preparation which has a sour flavour owing to the addition of lemon which is also recommended for the fish in the modernized version.

*F*RY THE tirrikh *and bone as mentioned. Sprinkle with seasonings. Break the egg over it and fry in sesame oil in a large frying pan. Keep stirring until browned as in the* mufarraka *dish mentioned previously. If desired sour, sprinkle with a little pure lemon juice.*

Sikbaj

Ingredients

1–1.25 kg./2–2½ lb. lamb shoulder
1 large onion
25 g./1 oz. fresh coriander, chopped
450 g./1 lb. leeks cut across in ½ pieces
1 small aubergine, about 225 g./8 oz.
50 g./2 oz. dried dates, chopped in half
50 g./2 oz. dried figs, chopped in half
25 g./1 oz. raisins
50 g./2 oz. blanched almond halves
1 tablespoon honey
250 ml./8 fl. oz. white wine vinegar
1 cinnamon stick
2 teaspoons coriander seeds, roasted and
  crushed
a few strands of saffron
2 tablespoons rosewater
salt to taste

1 Cut the lamb up into medium sized cubes and place in a heavy casserole together with the fresh coriander, cinnamon, and salt to taste. Cover with water and simmer for 45 minutes or until the meat is nearly tender. Remove scum if necessary.

2 Meanwhile chop the onion finely and slice the leeks. Peel and dice the aubergine and boil it in a separate pan for 10 minutes.

3 Add the onion and leeks to the casserole and simmer for 10 minutes; then add the aubergine and ground coriander and cook for a further 20 minutes.

4 Meanwhile prepare the wine vinegar by adding the saffron strands and honey to it, stirring until the mixture turns yellowish in colour. Add this to the casserole and stir in. Then place the dried fruit and almonds on the surface of the contents, cover the casserole and cook gently for a further 30 minutes. Add more stock if necessary.

5 Turn out onto a serving dish, arranging the fruit and nuts around the meat. Sprinkle with rosewater before serving.

Sikbaj. From the Persian for *sik* 'vinegar' and *baj* 'a kind, or sort of'. This thirteenth century version has an ancestry dating back to pre-Islamic times. It is related that the Sassanian Persian emperor (Chosroes Anushirwan) once tested a number of cooks, demanding that each of them prepare the finest dish he knew. Independently of each other, the only dish made was *sikbaj*. The emperor dubbed it 'the Queen of dishes' and paid each day one thousand silver coins to have it prepared. The dish was so highly prized that only those resident in the royal palace were permitted to enjoy it. A variety of this dish was prepared for and at the specific request of Ibrahim's nephew, the Caliph al-Amin, by Ibrahim's concubine and culinary collaborator, the remarkable Bid'a. A later version suggests that the pot of *sikbaj* should be placed, covered, in the oven overnight so that it cooks very slowly.

*C*UT FAT MEAT *into middling pieces, place in the pot and cover with water, fresh coriander, cinnamon bark and salt to taste. When boiling, remove the froth and cream with a ladle and discard. Remove the fresh coriander and add dry coriander. Take white onions, Syrian leeks, and carrots if in season, or else aubergine. Skin, splitting the aubergine thoroughly and half stew in water in a separate pot. Then strain and leave in the pot on top of the meat. Add seasonings and salt to taste. When almost cooked, take wine vinegar and date juice or honey if preferred – date juice is the more suitable – and mix together so that the mixture is mid-way between sharp and sweet, then pour into the pot and boil for an hour. When ready to take off the fire, remove a little of the broth, bray into it saffron as required and pour back into the pot. Then take sweet almonds, peel, split and place on top of the pan, together with a few raisins, currants and dried figs. Cover for an hour to settle over the heat of the fire. Wipe the sides with a clean cloth and sprinkle rose water on top. When settled, remove.*

'Ukaika

Ingredients
450 g./1 lb. lamb shoulder, cut into
    2.5-cm./1-inch cubes
175 ml./6 fl. oz. goat or sheep yoghurt
2 large cloves of garlic
2 tablespoons olive oil
2 teaspoons ground coriander
2 teaspoons ground cumin
1 teaspoon ground cinnamon
1 teaspoon mastic crystals (optional)
salt and pepper to taste
half each of green and red pepper, chopped
    fine for garnish

1 Heat the oil and fry the meat until browned on all sides.
2 Cover the meat with water, add the mastic (if desired) and seasonings: coriander, cumin, cinnamon, salt and pepper and cook slowly until the juices have all but evaporated, about one hour.
3 Meanwhile finely chop the garlic and mix into the yoghurt. When the meat is done, add the yoghurt sauce to it and gently heat until the sauce is warmed through.
4 Turn into a serving dish and garnish with chopped red and green pepper.

'Ukaika. Among the various Arabic culinary works of the medieval period only al-Baghdadi seems to know a dish by this name, the meaning of which is obscure. It appears in a section on milk dishes although the precise meaning of Persian milk (*al-laban al-Farisi*) is unclear. Here it has been interpreted as a kind of yoghurt. While this is admittedly speculation, it does not appear to have detracted from the interesting flavour of the dish.

*T*AKE FRESH TAIL, *cut up and dissolve extracting the sediment. Then take fat meat, cut up small, and throw into the dissolved tail stirring until browned. Cover with water and a little salt and leave to cook and dry, until only the oil remains of the juices. Throw in dry coriander and cumin ground fine, cinnamon, brayed pepper and mastic. Keep stirring. Take Persian milk as required, to which ground garlic has been added, and throw into the pot leaving to boil. Now remove from the fire and leave the pot over a gentle fire until the milk coagulates, when the oil floating on the top is thrown away. Then sprinkle a little fine ground cinnamon. Wipe the sides of the pot with a clean cloth and remove.*

Maqluba

Ingredients
225 g./8 oz. lean minced lamb
75–100 g./3–4 oz. walnuts, chopped fine
1 teaspoon sumac
$\frac{1}{2}$ teaspoon ground coriander
$\frac{1}{2}$ teaspoon ground cumin
$\frac{1}{2}$ teaspoon ground cinnamon
1 teaspoon dried mint
1 egg, beaten lightly
2 tablespoons olive oil
1 teaspoon lemon juice
pinch of salt and pepper to taste

1 Mix together in a bowl the meat, all the seasonings, the egg and the lemon juice and knead thoroughly. Add the chopped walnuts and knead the mixture some more, ensuring the nuts are evenly distributed throughout the mixture. Next, shape the mixture into a large ball. Then pinch off small portions and form flat 'cakes' in the palm of the hands.
2 Heat the oil in a frying pan and fry the 'cakes' on both sides for three or four minutes each side or until they appear done. They can be eaten hot or cold.

Maqluba. The meaning of this is simply 'turned over' and can apply to a wide variety of dishes where the inversion of the contents in the pan, in this case like cooking a hamburger, is performed. It is taken from al-Baghdadi's cookbook.

*T*AKE AND SLICE *red meat, then chop with a large knife. Put into the mortar and pound as small as possible. Take fresh sumac, boil in water, wring out and strain. Into this place the minced meat, and boil until cooked, so that it has absorbed all the sumac water, though covered to twice its depth. Then remove from the pot and spray with a little lemon juice. Lay out to dry. Then sprinkle with fine ground seasonings, dry coriander, cumin, pepper and cinnamon and rub over it a few sprigs of dry mint. Take walnuts, grind coarse and add. Break eggs and throw in mixing well. Make into cakes, and fry in fresh sesame oil in a fine iron or copper frying pan. When one side is cooked, turn over on to the other side. Then remove.*

Barida

Ingredients
1 medium chicken (1.25–1.5 kg./2½–3 lb.),
    jointed
50 g./2 oz. ground almonds
25 g./1 oz. castor sugar
250 ml./8 fl oz. white wine vinegar or cider
100 ml./4 fl oz. white wine vinegar
1 tablespoon olive oil
2 teaspoons mustard powder or yellow
    mustard with seeds
a few strands of saffron, or ½ teaspoon
    turmeric
salt to taste
seeds of one pomegranate for garnish
cucumber cut into half moon shapes for
    garnish
black olives (optional)
25 g./1 oz. toasted almond halves (optional)

1 Place the chicken joints with the cup of wine vinegar or cider into a pan and simmer for 30 minutes.
2 Meanwhile put the ground almonds, sugar, mustard, saffron, salt, oil and the half cup of white wine vinegar in a blender and make into a fine sauce.
3 Take the chicken from the pan when cooked and, after allowing it to cool somewhat, remove the meat from the bone and cut into small pieces. Add half a cup from the remaining stock in the pan to the almond mixture and stir in thoroughly.
4 Place the chicken pieces into a shallow serving dish and pour over it the almond mixture, making sure all the chicken is coated well. Arrange the half-moon shaped cucumber pieces around the edge of the dish and sprinkle the pomegranate seeds onto the chicken. If pomegranates are not available, olives and toasted almond halves make a pleasing and appetizing garnish in addition to the cucumber.

Barida. This cold dish made from chicken was devised by Ibrahim ibn al-Mahdi. The recipe is expressed in poetic form, not surprising from a man who was not only a gourmand, but well known as a poet too. He describes the dish as perfect summertime fare. The physician al-Razi observes that such dishes of the *bawarid* type, when made with vinegar or with the juice of sour fruits, serve to cool the temperament and moderate it. *Qutha* and *faqqus*, mentioned in the original recipe, are species of cucumber.

*T*WO PARTS ALMONDS *and sugar and two parts vinegar and mustard mixed together in a vessel with partially dried safflower adding colour around the edges. Cucumber peeled,* qutha *and* faqqus *and pomegranate, chopped up small and sprinkled around the vessel. Add a little oil. Take a fine young chicken, cooked in vinegar, jointed and cut up in pieces and placed over the other ingredients in the vessel. Decorate the dish with pomegranate (seeds) and with almonds and olives chopped up fine.*

Narjisiya

Ingredients

450 g./1 lb. shoulder or leg of lamb, cut into
    2.5 cm./1-inch cubes
2 medium onions, chopped fine
3 large spring onions, chopped
8 spears cooked asparagus (fresh or tinned)
3 tablespoons olive oil
4 egg yolks
15 g./$\frac{1}{2}$ oz. coarsely chopped fresh coriander
2 teaspoons ground coriander
1 teaspoon ground cinnamon
1 teaspoon ground cumin
$\frac{1}{2}$ teaspoon sumac
$\frac{1}{2}$ teaspoon ground ginger
salt and pepper to taste
few sprigs of fresh rue as garnish (optional)

1 Heat the oil and fry the meat until sealed.
2 Add the ground coriander, cumin, salt and cinnamon and coat the meat in the spices. Then add the onion, spring onion and fresh coriander and fry gently a further 5 minutes.
3 Cover with water and simmer for an hour allowing the liquid to reduce considerably but not entirely dry out. Add the ginger, sumac and pepper.
4 Turn into a sauté dish or shallow cast iron dish and arrange the cooked asparagus so that they radiate from the centre.
5 Place the intact egg yolks carefully at equal intervals between the asparagus spears. Return to a low heat, cover the dish and cook very gently until the yolks are just done but not solid. Garnish with sprigs of rue if desired. Serve immediately.

Narjisiya. This is Ibrahim ibn al-Mahdi in poetic flight again, where he is replying to a friend's request for the recipe for a fine dish. A surprising ingredient is asparagus which but rarely appears in these recipes, although Ibrahim seemed to have a particular liking for it (see recipe on page 94). In a later recipe from al-Baghdadi's work, the narcissus flower is imitated by garnishing the dish with poached eggs, evidence that attention was paid as well to the presentation of the dishes on the table.

R EMOVE THE CHOPS *from the carcass and then the meat and fat of the flank.* *Cut up the fresh fat meat and wash it. Place it in a vessel over the fire and fry it in oil and spices until browned. Then cut up over it onion round and fresh green onion and add rue and coriander. Then add* murri, *ginger and a little pepper. Next add asparagus. Break over this egg yolks which resemble the radiant stars of the firmament and the rounded shaped flower of narcissus. Sprinkle bits of rue over the top. Then, remember God and eat this delicious wholesome food.*

Tabahija

Ingredients
450 g./1 lb. leg of lamb, sliced into thin strips
450 g./1 lb. aubergine, peeled and sliced
225 g./8 oz. onion, sliced
5 tablespoons olive oil
100 ml./4 fl. oz. white wine vinegar
2 tablespoons sumac juice (optional)
2 teaspoons ground cumin
3 teaspoons roasted ground coriander seeds
2 teaspoons roasted ground caraway seeds
2 teaspoons ground cinnamon
salt to taste
sprigs of fresh parsley for garnish

1 Heat the oil and fry the meat until sealed.
2 Add the onion, aubergine and salt and cook for a further 10 minutes.
3 Cover with water and simmer for 45 minutes or until the meat is tender.
4 Add the vinegar, sumac juice if desired. (See step 2 in the method for 'Ijja min Badhinjan, p. 00 for preparation of sumac juice) and the spices and cook for a further 15 minutes.
5 Turn into a serving dish and garnish with sprigs of parsley or other fresh herbs such as mint or coriander.

Tabahija. Another dish whose name is Arabicized from the Persian. There are also many varieties of this dish which appear in most of the culinary manuals. This one, attributed to Ibrahim ibn al-Mahdi, is the earliest one we have. Like _murri_, _kamakh_ is a savoury seasoning which is time-consuming to prepare, the operation commencing in June and ending in October. In this preparation for _Tabahija_, _kamakh_ juice is used which means extracting the soluble elements from it by steeping or soaking in water. A later, thirteenth century, version of this dish suggests sumac juice, prepared in the same way as _kamakh_ juice as a substitute for _murri_.

*T*AKE THE MEAT *and slice and wash it thoroughly. Put half a ratl of water in a pot and boil it. Place the meat in the pot and pour over it fine oil, a little salt and cut up into it peeled aubergine and onion rings. When the contents have cooked and the liquid evaporated, sprinkle over it the amount of half a spoonful of kamakh juice and murri, and if desired, an equal amount of vinegar. Next proceed to chop up some herbs and spices, a little each of coriander or caraway, cinnamon and cumin, sprinkle over the contents and stir a while. Wash the sides of the pot with a ladle of water and leave awhile until settled. Then serve, God willing.*

Zaitun

Ingredients
225 g./8 oz. black olives, washed to remove
  the brine
250 ml./8 fl. oz. olive oil
1½ teaspoons dried thyme
salt to taste

1 Mix all the ingredients together in a lidded jar and leave for several days or longer before serving.

Zaitun. This way of preparing and storing olives, suggested by Ibrahim ibn al-Mahdi, provides a pleasant side dish placed alongside others on the meal table to be dipped into when desired. They can also be used wherever olives are called for in the recipes (eg. recipe on page 56). The Mediterranean region provides 98% of the world's acreage of olive production used to make oil. The vegetable, which is native to that area, has been cultivated for three millenia for cooking, lamp and cosmetic oils and for food.

*T*AKE BLACK OR GREEN OLIVES, *black being the best and put them in a jar adding to the contents salt and thyme. Then cover with fine oil. Use when the occasion arises, God willing.*

'Ijja min Badhinjan

Ingredients   Makes 18 portions
450 g./1 lb. aubergine
1 teaspoon coriander seeds, roasted and
    ground
$\frac{1}{2}$ teaspoon freshly ground pepper
$\frac{1}{2}$ teaspoon ground cinnamon
250 ml./8 fl. oz. golden or wholewheat
    breadcrumbs
100 ml./4 fl. oz. red wine vinegar
1 tablespoon olive oil
2 cloves garlic, finely crushed
1 teaspoon sumac
oil for frying

1 Peel the aubergine, cut into quarters and
boil in plain water until soft. Drain the water
off thoroughly. Place in a bowl and extract
the excess moisture with kitchen towels.
2 Meanwhile prepare the *murri* substitute
which involves merely putting the sumac in
a half cup of water and boiling it for about
three minutes to reduce the liquid by half.
Set aside in a small container.

3 Add the breadcrumbs, pepper, coriander,
cinnamon and one teaspoon of the *murri*
substitute to the aubergine and vigorously
blend together until the mixture is smooth.
4 Heat some oil in a frying pan and shallow
fry over a medium heat tablespoon sized
amounts of the aubergine mixture. This can
be done easily by flattening the mixture on
the spoon and gently easing it with the
fingers into the frying pan. Allow the 'loaves'
to brown on one side before turning them
over.
5 Prepare the sauce from the vinegar, olive
oil, garlic and two teaspoons of the *murri*
substitute. Boil together in a pan until the
liquid has been reduced by about half.
6 Serve the 'loaves' on a plate and put the
sauce in a separate small vessel to
accompany them. The aubergine can then
be eaten with or without the sauce, either
way being delicious.

'Ijja min Badhinjan. The customary form of *'ijja* is a food made with eggs,
like an omelette (see recipe on page 110). Here the word is used in another,
known, sense to apply to a dish compounded of different ingredients mixed
into a kind of dough and fried. The binding agent in this preparation is
provided by the breadcrumbs rather than the egg. This recipe is from an
anonymous work of probable Egyptian origin.

*T*AKE A PLEASANT AUBERGINE *and peel it. Boil it in salted water until it is cooked through. Extract from it all the moisture. Then, knead it in a bowl with crumbled pieces of bread with an infusion of* murri, *pepper, dried coriander and cinnamon and beat them all together until the mixture is smooth. Then fry in a pan with oil, small loaf-sized portions of the mixture until cooked and browned. Make a sauce of vinegar and oil and* murri *and crushed garlic. Boil these together and pour over the loaves when ready for eating.*

Jazr

450 g./1 lb. carrots, diced
1 tablespoon olive oil
100 ml./4 fl. oz. red wine vinegar
1 clove garlic, crushed
1 teaspoon caraway seeds
salt to taste

1 Cut the carrots lengthwise in half and then in quarters and cut the sticks into 1-cm/ ½-inch pieces. Boil for 5 minutes in salted water. Drain the water from the pan, remove the carrots and set aside.
2 Heat the oil in the pan and replace the carrots, stirring them for a further 5 minutes. Remove when cooked, but still crisp.
3 Put the vinegar, crushed garlic and caraway seeds in the pan and bring to the boil until the liquid is reduced by half. Return the carrots to the pan and stir into the mixture.

Jazr. There are few dishes in the medieval Arabic repertoire where a vegetable is highlighted by itself. In this case it is used to decorate the plate on which something else is served; it is, in fact, a perfect accompaniment with a dish of plain rice. Carrots, at least, can be treated on their own as the carrot family of plants (which includes caraway, cumin, coriander, and dill, all common to medieval Arab cooking) is characterised by strongly scented essential oils. This recipe is thirteenth century Moroccan.

*C*UT THE CARROTS *into pieces without peeling them. Select the middle bits and cut each piece in half and cook in salted water. Dry the pieces off and fry in a pan with fresh oil. Then pour over it boiling vinegar with crushed garlic and caraway. One can either leave the carrot pieces without frying (or else place them after frying) as decoration on a platter.*

Maghmuma

Ingredients
675 g./1½ lb. lamb, diced into small cubes
2 chicken livers, chopped
4 spring onions, finely chopped
100 g./4 oz. chopped leeks
175 g./6 oz. cooked chickpeas (tinned)
10–12 spears of fresh, tinned or frozen
  asparagus
2 tablespoons olive oil
50 g./2 oz. ground walnuts
100 g./4 oz. goat's or sheep's cheese,
  chopped fine
6–8 black olives, stoned and cut in half
1 egg
25 g./1 oz. coarsely chopped fresh coriander
2 teaspoons ground coriander
1 teaspoon sumac
salt to taste
2 loaves of Arabic bread
oil for frying the bread

1 Liquidize the cooked chickpeas to a paste.
2 Boil the asparagus spears in lightly salted water and cook until tender. Drain the asparagus, remove and cut each one into two. Reserve to the end and use as a garnish.
3 Into a heavy casserole place the meat, chicken livers, oil, onions, leeks, fresh coriander, one teaspoon ground coriander, salt to taste and the ground chickpeas. Cover the contents with water, mix thoroughly and simmer for an hour. Add more water if necessary.
4 Meanwhile cut up the loaves of bread into 3.5-cm./1½-inch squares and fry in a pan until crisp and brown.
5 When the casserole contents are ready add the cheese and walnuts, mixing in well and cook gently for another 10 minutes.
6 Beat the egg lightly in a bowl adding the other teaspoon of ground coriander, and the sumac. Stir this into the casserole until the egg is cooked.
7 Place the fried bread squares on the bottom of a serving dish and turn the contents of the casserole over the bread, arranging the asparagus in a pattern on top.

Maghmuma. The word means simply 'covered', in reference to the bread covering of the pot at the end of the preparation. Another version of this dish is made in several layers, each one 'covering' the other. This particular recipe was devised by Ibrahim ibn al-Mahdi.

*T*AKE FRESH AND TENDER *asparagus and boil lightly, then cut up into small pieces and remove. Take meat and cut up into small pieces. Next from a chicken, remove the fat, the gizzard and liver and after cleaning, add them to the pot, except the liver which may be put in last. Pour over this washed oil and crushed chick peas, ground salt, white of onion fresh coriander and leeks all chopped up. Pour in water just less than enough to cover the contents and boil until cooked. When cooked, add the asparagus with chopped walnuts, chopped cheese and pitted olives adding as well dried coriander and pepper. Take an egg and break it into a dish adding to it also pepper and coriander. Beat vigorously. (The cheese and olives have already been added to the pot before the egg is poured over top and stirred in.) Add also some* murri *and cook until the contents dry out. Next take a bread loaf and cut round it so that it is the size of the pot and fry it in oil until done. Then place it over the meat and spices in the pot. If you wish, when emptying the pot, ladle the contents onto the bread and serve. God willing.*

Tuffahiya

Ingredients
450 g./1 lb. lamb or chicken, diced
1 large cooking apple (about 225 g./8 oz.),
   peeled, cored and diced
2 teaspoons olive oil
1 teaspoon coriander seeds, roasted and
   crushed
1 teaspoon dried mint
1 large onion (about 225 g./8 oz.), sliced
   finely
50 g./2 oz. almond halves or flaked almonds
1 cinnamon stick
1 teaspoon ground cinnamon
1½ teaspoons ground ginger
salt and pepper to taste
olives or chopped red and green pepper for
   garnish

1 Heat the oil in a pan and add the meat,
coriander and a pinch of salt. Cook the meat
until browned all over.
2 Add half the onion, cinnamon bark,
ginger, mint and pepper to taste. Cover with
water, bring to the boil and cook for 30
minutes. Remove the cinnamon bark.
3 Next add the apple, almonds, the ground
cinnamon, and the rest of the onion and
cook for a further 30 minutes or until the
meat is tender. Turn out into a serving dish
and garnish with olives or chopped red and
green peppers.

Tuffahiya. Named after the characteristic ingredient, apple (*tuffah*). The
organic acid characteristic of cooking apples is malic acid and in this recipe
it is subtly offset by the ground almonds. cinnamon and ginger. From the
thirteenth century work of al-Baghdadi.

*T*AKE FAT MEAT *and cut into small strips. Throw into the pot with a little salt and dry coriander and boil until almost cooked. Remove and throw away the scum. Cut up onions small and throw in with cinnamon bark, pepper, mastic and ginger ground fine and a few sprigs of mint. Take sour apples, remove the pips, and pound in a stone mortar, squeezing out the juice. Put in on top of the meat. Peel almonds and soak in water, then throw in. Kindle the fire under it until the whole is done, then leave over the fire to settle. If desired add a chicken, cutting it into quarters and letting it cook with the meat. Then remove.*

Aruzz mufalfal

Ingredients
175 g./6 oz. lean minced lamb or beef
$\frac{1}{2}$ teaspoon each of dried coriander, cumin
    and cinnamon; $\frac{1}{4}$ teaspoon of each spice
1 tablespoon olive oil
500 ml./17 fl. oz. rice
1 piece cinnamon bark
salt to taste
1 teaspoon olive oil
$\frac{1}{4}$ teaspoon turmeric
1200 ml./2 pints water
25 g./1 oz. roasted almonds or pine seeds for
    garnish

1 Heat the tablespoon of oil and adding half a teaspoon of dried coriander, cumin and cinnamon together with the meat, and fry until brown all over. Remove and sprinkle over top another $\frac{1}{4}$ teaspoon of the same spices.

2 Boil lightly salted water in a saucepan with a teaspoon of oil and cinnamon bark for about 5 minutes. Then add the rice and turmeric and simmer gently in the pan, covered, for about 15 minutes, ensuring that the water has not been completely absorbed; add a little if it has been.

3 Add the minced meat on top of the rice, cover the pan and cook for another 5 minutes or so.

4 Serve the rice and meat mixed together on a plate. Garnish with roasted almonds or pine seeds.

Aruzz mufallfal. Plain rice dishes, as we know them, are not found in the cooking manuals which may appear surprising given its widespread consumption in medieval times. Possibly this is just a hint of the fact that rice was regarded as poor man's fare. More likely, however, is that rice was used as a thickening agent in other dishes, or cooked with milk and meat as in Ibrahim ibn al-Mahdi's recipe for *Aruzziya*. This one is taken from the later cookbook of al-Baghdadi, and comes closest to what today would be recognized as the usual preparation of rice.

*T*AKE FAT MEAT and cut into middling pieces. Dissolve fresh tail and throw away the sediment. Pour in the meat and stir until browned. Sprinkle with a little salt and dry coriander ground fine. Then cover with water and boil until cooked, throwing away the scum. Remove from the pan when the water has dried and it is itself juicy, and not absolutely parched. Throw in dry coriander, cumin, cinnamon and mastic brayed fine, as required, and likewise salt. When quite cooked, remove from the pan, draining off the water and oil and sprinkle with the seasonings mentioned. Now take a kail of rice and three and a half kails of water. Dissolve fresh tail, about one third the weight of the meat. Pour water into the pan, and when boiling, throw in the melted fat, add mastic and cinnamon bark and bring thoroughly to the boil. Wash the rice several times, colour with saffron, and place in the water without stirring. Then cover the pan for a while until the rice swells and the water boils. Now remove the cover, and lay the meat in strips on top of the rice and cover again, placing a cloth over the cover, wrapping it up so that no air can get in. Leave the pan to settle over a gentle fire for a while. Then remove. Some make it simple, without the saffron colouring.

Samak summaqiya

Ingredients
675–900 g./1½–2 lb. white fish of any kind,
   cut into large pieces
2 large onions, chopped fine
3–4 tablespoons olive oil
2 cloves garlic, crushed
2 teaspoons coriander seeds, roasted and
   crushed
1 teaspoon ground coriander
2 teaspoons sumac
½ teaspoon fresh ground black pepper
2 tablespoons sesame paste (*tahina*)
juice of one lemon or more according to
   taste
50 g./2 oz. roasted ground hazelnuts

1 Heat the olive oil in a frying pan and add the roasted ground coriander seeds. Fry the fish pieces on both sides until cooked. Remove the fish from the pan and set aside. Add some more oil, if necessary, to the pan for the next step.

2 Add to the frying pan the onion, garlic, ground coriander, sumac, pepper and fry until the onion is golden. Mix the lemon juice with the sesame paste and stir this into the onion and cook for a further 5 minutes. Add more water if the mixture appears to become too thick.

3 Place the fish pieces on a serving dish, and place the cooked onion around it. Sprinkle the roasted hazelnuts over the plate and serve.

Samak summaqiya. This recipe comes from the anonymous work which is in all probability of Egyptian provenance. The dish takes its name from the spice sumac which comes from the fruits of a wild Mediterranean bush, the best qualities growing at altitude in rocky, mountainous areas away from the coasts. The fruits are dried, crushed and sieved, forming a coarse-grained purple-red powder, the process alluded to in the recipe itself. Sumac has a pleasant astringency owing to malic acid and is used as a souring agent in place of lemon or vinegar.

*O*NE REQUIRES FRESH FISH, *sumac, sesame seed paste, garlic, pepper, onion, dried coriander, lemon (or candied lemon peel), hazelnuts and sesame oil. Mince the onion fine and fry it in oil. Sieve the sumac, grinding it and processing it twice through the sieve until its effective properties have been extracted. Then place the minced onion in a pan and grind in all the other ingredients, adding over it the sesame seed paste and the juice of lemon from which the seeds have been removed. Heat until the mixture has boiled. Wash the fish, cut into large pieces and add to the pan, boiling until done. Place the contents in a vessel. Roast some hazelnuts and grind them adding them to the surface of the dish and then serve.*

'Ashiqa

Ingredients

450 g./1 lb. chicken breasts, cut into slices
450 g./1 lb. lean lamb, minced fine
1 tin (about 400 g./14 oz.) chick-peas
1 small onion, chopped finely
1 medium onion, chopped coarsely
100 g./4 oz. fresh spinach, chopped coarsely
15 g./½ oz. fresh coriander leaves, chopped
  finely
25 g./1 oz. fresh coriander, leaves and stocks
  chopped coarsely
2 teaspoons dried ground coriander
2 teaspoons cinnamon
25 g./1 oz. each of almonds, walnuts and
  pistachio nuts, chopped coarsely
50 g./2 oz. ground almonds
2 tablespoons olive oil
oil for frying
300 ml./½ pint unsweetened white grape
  juice
salt and pepper to taste

1 Into a bowl put the chopped and ground nuts and the grape juice and let this sit until ready for use towards the end of the preparation.

2 Put 25 g./1 oz. fresh coriander leaves and stocks and the chopped medium sized onion into a pot with about 1.5 litres/2 pints of water and boil uncovered for 20 minutes or so until the liquid is reduced by half. Strain the stock into a heavy casserole.

3 Place the chicken slices into the casserole along with the chick-peas, the spinach, a bit of salt and pepper and a tablespoon of the olive oil. Cover and cook gently for 30 minutes.

4 Meanwhile, blend together the minced lamb, the small chopped onion, the chopped fresh coriander leaves, the dried ground coriander, some pepper, the cinnamon and the second tablespoon of olive oil. Knead the mixture well and then form small cabobs from it by pinching off walnut sized amounts and rolling them in the palms of the hands. Fry these in ordinary oil until browned all over.

5 Pour the nuts and grape juice mixture into the casserole. Then carefully lay the fried cabobs on the surface of the contents and cook for another 30 minutes. Turn the contents of the casserole into a serving bowl and arrange the cabobs around the edge and serve.

'Ashiqa. This is one of Ibrahim's preparations belonging to a group of dishes called 'lover' or 'beloved' (ma'shuqa) referring to the female of the pair. It is perhaps the most subtle of all his dishes with a wide range of flavours and aromatic nuances.

*C*UT UP BUSTARD, *or duck or chicken. Then wash and clean the bird. Put in a pot with oil and chickpeas and salt. Onion and fresh coriander are both chopped up and boiled and then the stock is poured over the contents of the pot and cooked. Pound the meat of the leg very fine together with fresh and dried coriander and onion and a little pepper and cinnamon. When the fowl is cooked, the ground up ingredients are thrown in. Grind up almonds, walnuts and pistachios together mixed with the juice of unripe grapes and throw in. If you desire to put in spinach or sarmaq, then do so.*

Hais

Ingredients
225 g./8 oz. cooking dates, cut up
175 g./6 oz. digestive biscuits, powdered
50 g./2 oz. shelled pistachios, chopped fine
50 g./2 oz. ground almonds
2 tablespoons sesame seed oil
castor or granulated sugar as required

1 If the dates are very solid, you will need to soften them up by placing them in a pan with a little water and heating them gently while mashing them with a wooden spoon.
2 Mix together all the ingredients and knead well into one large ball. Then pinch off small portions of the mixture and roll in the palms of the hands forming bite-sized balls. Place them next in a container which has sugar spread across the bottom and shake the balls around so they become thoroughly coated with the sugar. Keep in the refrigerator until ready to use.

Hais. A sweetmeat of ancient ancestry, eaten wherever dates were plentiful and perhaps almost the only staple food. *Hais* is said to have been served at the wedding dinner when the Prophet Muhammad married Safiya. Commonly the dish was prepared by mixing dates with clarified butter (*samn*) and dried curd (*'iqt*). The recipe here is taken from al-Baghdadi and reflects the transformation of this essentially poor-man's dish to suit middle class urban tastes in its use of nuts and sesame oil. As it lasted well, it was convenient and nourishing for travellers to take a supply with them on their journeys.

*T*AKE FINE DRY BREAD, *or biscuit and grind up well. Take a* ratl *of this and three quarters of fresh or preserved dates with the stones removed, together with three* uqiya *of ground almonds and pistachios. Knead all together very well with the hands. Refine two* uqiya *of sesame oil and pour over, working with the hand until it is mixed in. Make into cabobs and dust with fine-ground sugar. If desired, instead of sesame oil use butter. This is excellent for travellers.*

Mutajjana Ibrahimya

Ingredients
675 g./1½ lb. chicken meat, chopped fine or
   minced
1 large onion (about 225 g./8 oz.) chopped
   fine
6 large eggs, beaten
675 g./1½ lb. buttom mushrooms, sliced
25 g./1 oz. fresh coriander, chopped
1 tablespoon fresh mint chopped, or 1
   teaspoon dried mint
1 teaspoon ground cinnamon
½ teaspoon ground ginger
½ teaspoon ground coriander
½ teaspoon sumac
vinegar
a few strands of saffron or ½ teaspoon
   turmeric
4 tablespoons olive oil
pepper to taste

1 Mix the chicken, onion and half the fresh coriander together thoroughly until you have a coarse pasty substance. Press this onto the bottom of a heavy casserole and flatten it out so that it resembles a large meatburger. Cover this with a half-vinegar, half-water stock, adding two tablespoons of oil and the saffron or turmeric, to just above the level of the 'cake'. Bring to the boil and simmer for about 30 minutes, or until the chicken appears done. Remove from the heat.
2 Fry the sliced mushrooms in the remaining two tablespoons of oil for about 5 minutes and then add the ground coriander, cinnamon, ginger, and sumac and stir in well for another 5 minutes. Add this mixture carefully over the chicken in the pan.
3 Beat the eggs lightly in a bowl and add the remaining fresh coriander, the mint and pepper to taste. Return the pan to the heat and pour the eggs over the contents. Cover the pan and allow it to simmer gently until the eggs are just done.

Mutajjana Ibrahimiya. This preparation, attributed to Ibrahim ibn al-Mahdi, is a variation of a recipe which was a favourite of Ibrahim's great nephew, the Caliph al-Wathiq who is also said to have compiled a cookbook. It is unusual for the layered effect it is supposed to achieve.

TAKE ONE KASKARI chicken or two young birds, remove all their meat and from it make a thin cake and place it in a pot. With the meat add a third of a ratl of chopped onion and a half uqiya of chopped fresh coriander. Pour over this water to cover it to twice its depth, a third of a ratl of pleasant oil and salt as required. Place the pot on the fire until it comes well to the boil. Next take truffles, of a variety suitable, as much as the weight of the meat and cut them up in a fashion thicker than the cake and fry in the pot until everything therein is cooked. Then add an amount of dried coriander which the finger tips together can hold, pepper the weight of one dirhem, ginger and galingal of each half a dirhem and cinnamon a dirhem. Stir. Take fifteen eggs, break them into a vessel and beat them together with some fresh coriander and mint, both chopped. Then pour into the pot and stir until the egg has broken up and mixed with the cake and the truffles. Wash the sides of the pot and cover it until required. Let the eggs be poured into the pot only after it has been removed from the fire but before the boiling has entirely ceased.

Another preparation called Ibrahimi is made in the above manner except that in it there is half a ratl of vinegar mixed with a dirhem's weight of saffron. There is no salt except half a dirhem's weight and there is a quarter ratl of murri al-Razi. The remainder of the preparation is as above.

'Adasiya

Ingredients
225 g./8 oz. brown or green lentils, soaked
    an hour in hot water
1 medium onion, chopped fine
225 g./8 oz. lean lamb, chopped into small
    pieces
2 tablespoons olive oil
1 large clove garlic, crushed
15 g./$\frac{1}{2}$ oz. fresh coriander, coarsely chopped
1 teaspoon coriander seeds
1 teaspoon ground cumin
100 g./4 oz. feta cheese, chopped fine
100 ml./4 fl. oz. wine or cider vinegar

1 Heat the oil in a frying pan and add the meat, onion and garlic. Stir until the meat is browned all over and then simmer for 5 minutes.

2 Drain the water from the lentils and put into a heavy casserole, together with the fried meat, onion and garlic, adding just enough fresh water to cover the contents. Bring back to the boil, partially cover the casserole and cook for half an hour or until the lentils are tender. Allow the water to reduce somewhat while being careful not to let the contents burn.

3 Roast the coriander seeds and grind in a mortar together with the cumin. Add to the casserole along with the fresh coriander, vinegar and the cheese. Stir the mixture thoroughly and simmer gently for a further 30 minutes. This dish can either be served hot or enjoyed cold.

'Adasiya. This dish is found in the earliest culinary manual compiled, by al-Warraq. Named for its chief ingredient, the lentil (*'adas*), which is probably the oldest cultivated legume and is native to southwest Asia, possibly northern Syria and Iraq. The original recipe calls for the inclusion of meat, but it can be prepared as well without for those with vegetarian preferences. A variation of this recipe suggests using beet root which could be substituted for the fresh coriander.

YOU COOK THE MEAT with chopped onion in oil and when the pot has been brought to the boil, and the scum removed, husked lentils are thrown in and cooked thoroughly. Then you pour in vinegar and spice it with coriander and cumin; throw in garlic (as well). Whosoever wishes may throw in ground cheese; whosoever wishes may colour it yellow with saffron. Throw in beet root without the cheese and garlic. Whosoever wishes may throw in something sweet.

'Ijja Mu'tamidiya

Ingredients
225 g./8 oz. chicken breast, diced fine
225 g./8 oz. minced lamb
100 g./4 oz. feta or Lancashire cheese, sliced
  fine
4 eggs
1 tablespoon olive oil
1 teaspoon coriander
1 teaspoon cinnamon
1 teaspoon sumac
10 black olives, quartered
freshly ground pepper to taste
a few sprigs of rue (optional)

1 Heat the oil in a non-stick frying pan, add the chicken and the meat and cook the meat through for about 20 minutes.
2 Add the coriander, cinnamon and sumac and half the cheese to the pan and cook for a further 10 minutes.
3 Meanwhile, beat the eggs lightly in a bowl and add the olives. When the meat is ready, spoon it into the egg mixture and stir well, coating the meat thoroughly. Add the freshly ground pepper to taste.
4 Tip the mixture carefully back into the frying pan and cook over a medium heat until the bottom is done. Then cover the pan with a plate, turning it over to empty the omelette onto the plate. Gently edge the half done omelette back into the pan and finish cooking the other side. Turn out onto a clean plate and allow to cool a little before cutting up into serving portions. If rue is available, cut up a few sprigs and sprinkle over the top as garnish.

'Ijja Mu'tamidiya. This recipe for medieval omelette has been taken from what is likely the only surviving Egyptian culinary work which is, however, anonymous and undated. The recipe is named after someone called *Mu'tamid,* a name carried by a number of Caliphs or wazirs. The physician al-Razi recommends using oil in the cooking of omelettes rather than clarified butter (*samn*) because oil is lighter and makes the food easier to digest. He also suggests using only the egg yolks rather than the whites, again for the sake of digestion.

*T*AKE THE BREASTS *of two young fowl and slice the meat finely; take a* ratl *of meat and slice it similarly. Wash the meat and put it into a pot on the fire. Pour a* ratl *of oil into the pot and two dirhems of salt. Boil until nearly cooked. Then take a quarter* ratl *of cheese, slice it, and add it to the pot with the meat. Season with two dirhems of dried coriander and a dirhem each of pepper and cinnamon. Add ten olives, pitted. Break into a container twenty eggs and pour an* uqiya *of* murri *over them, beating them vigorously. Stir the contents of the pot and leave on the fire until firm. Then pour over it the egg. Chop up some rue over it. Remove and serve.*

Aruzziya

Ingredients

225 g./8 oz. smoked beef or lamb, cut into
    thin strips
225 g./8 oz. fatty portion of lamb shoulder,
    diced small
1 tablespoon olive oil
600 ml./1 pint skimmed milk
225 g./8 oz. Basmati rice
1 cinnamon stick
2–3 small pieces root ginger, peeled
$\frac{1}{2}$ teaspoon ground cinnamon
salt to taste
olives or green and red pepper for garnish

1 Wash the rice thoroughly in cold water
until the water leaving it is clear.
2 Add the ginger pieces and cinnamon stick
to the milk in a pan and bring to the boil.
Set aside for half an hour to allow the spices
to infuse into the milk.
3 Heat the oil in a frying pan, add the pieces
of lamb shoulder and cook until brown and
crisp. Then add the smoked meat and fry 2
or 3 minutes. Remove from the heat and set
aside.
4 Remove the ginger and cinnamon from
the milk and add to it the washed rice, salt
to taste and ground cinnamon. Simmer,
stirring frequently until the rice is cooked.
Add a little water if the rice dries out so as to
have some liquid left when the rice is
cooked.
5 Add the meat and any oil remaining in the
pan and mix thoroughly into the rice.
Remove from the heat, cover and let stand a
quarter of an hour. Then, 5 minutes before
serving set on a very low heat. Turn out into
a serving dish and garnish as you wish.

Aruzziya. Rice cooked in milk seems plain enough, but with the additional
flavours of the smoked beef and the fatty pieces of lamb, this dish is one of
Ibrahim ibn al-Mahdi's more unusual creations. The curing of meat by
smoking was an operation often performed in the domestic kitchen. Here
the intention seems to be less a process of slow, low-temperature cooking
than a complex chemical treatment of the meat by smoke which is finished
off by means of frying.

*T*AKE RED MEAT *from the lower thighs and also from the tail fat and cut both into fine thin slices. Then smoke the meat until it is well done. Next take a pot and pour oil into it and when sizzling, throw into it the tail and the smoked meat and fry until cooked. Then sprinkle salt and water over it but do not use* murri *so as not to spoil it. Next, take a large pot and pour fresh milk into it half full and boil. When at the boil throw in a stick of galingal, cinnamon and salt as much as needed. Then take the rice and wash it very well and add it to the milk. When cooked through take the fried meat and its oil, add to the pot and stir in vigorously and serve. God willing.*

Mubazzar

Ingredients

450 g./1 lb. lean lamb, cut into 2.5-cm./
    1-inch cubes
100 ml./4 fl. oz. red wine vinegar
1 teaspoon coriander seed, roasted and then
    ground together with
2 teaspoons ground cumin and
1 teaspoon ground cinnamon
salt to taste
wedges of lemon as garnish

1 Put the meat together with the vinegar and a pinch of salt in a pan, uncovered, and simmer gently for half an hour.
2 Mix the spices together and add them to the meat when it is ready, turning the pieces over to ensure that they become coated with the spices.
3 Cover the pan and place it in a medium oven (190C, 375F, Gas Mark 5) for another half hour.
4 Turn into a serving dish and garnish with lemon wedges.

Mubazzar. Literally, this dish means 'seasoned with spices' (*abazir*). The effect of the preparation is to make spicy, but somewhat dry, pieces of meat which go well either with a rice accompaniment or mixed in with the rice itself. A recipe of Ibrahim ibn al-Mahdi.

TAKE A SIDE OF LAMB and stew it in good strong vinegar until it is half done. Remove from the fire and leave it in its vinegar until it has cooled off. Then remove the meat from the vinegar and firmly express its juices. Then throw over it coriander, cumin, pepper and cinnamon each ground. Then lower the meat into the oven and leave until it has lost its moisture.

Fustaqiya

Ingredients
675 g./1½ lb. chicken breasts
50 g./2 oz. pistachio nuts ground fine
50 g./2 oz. ground almonds
15 g./½ oz. sugar
15 g./½ oz. whole pistachio nuts for garnish

1 Boil the chicken in slightly salted water for about 15 minutes.
2 Remove the chicken and cut into small pieces. Add the pieces to fresh water in the pan, barely covering the meat, and add the ground nuts and sugar. Cook for half an hour over a slow heat.
3 Turn onto a serving dish and garnish with the whole pistachio nuts.

Fustaqiya. This dish takes its name from the pistachio nut (*fustuq*). A very simple dish to prepare, it comes from the early collection of recipes compiled by al-Warraq. The pistachio nut, which is native to Iraq and Iran, is a relative of the cashew, which might be substituted if pistachios are not readily available.

*T*AKE THE BREASTS OF CHICKENS, *and half boil in water and a little salt. Drain off the water, and take the flesh off the bones, pulling it into threads. Then put back into the saucepan, covering with water. Take peeled pistachios as required, and pound in the mortar. Put into the saucepan and stir, boiling. When almost cooked, throw in as much sugar as the pistachios. Keep stirring until set; then remove.*

Bustaniya

Ingredients

450 g./1 lb. chicken breasts, cut into thin
  slices
225 g./8 oz. lamb, diced into small pieces
100 g./4 oz. dried pears, soaked in two cups
  hot water
100 g./4 oz. dried peaches
pepper to taste
1½ teaspoons ground ginger
1 teaspoon ground cinnamon
1 tablespoon sugar
250 ml./8 fl. oz. white wine vinegar
25 g./1 oz. ground almonds
2 eggs, lightly beaten

1 Soak the pears in the hot water for about
half an hour. Pour the water (but not the
pears) into a pot and add the chicken and
meat; season with pepper to taste. Cover,
and boil gently for half and hour.
2 Add the peaches, ginger, cinnamon, sugar,
vinegar and ground almonds and cook
gently, covered, for another 30 minutes,
adding a little water if the contents appear to
be drying out.
3 Add the beaten eggs to the contents of the
pot and fold in gently, leaving it over a low
heat until the egg has set.
4 Turn out onto a serving dish and garnish
the plate with the soaked pears cut in half.

Bustaniya. This is a preparation of one Abu Samin about whom nothing is
known for certain but who may have been a professional chef in the
employ of the Caliph al-Wathiq. If so, Ibrahim ibn al-Mahdi would surely
have known of his skills. His name which means 'Father of Corpulence', or
'obesity' if one is being less kind, seems appropriate to his profession. The
dish is named not after any particular ingredient, as was the custom, but
after the orchard (*bustan*) from which the selection of fruits was made.

TAKE SMALL SOUR PEARS, wash and wrap in a moist cloth if they are dried pears, but if they are fresh, then macerate them in water and strain through a sieve. Then take chicken breasts, and cut them lengthwise into finger-sized strips and add to it as much meat as you wish. Next throw in peaches and boil (with the meat). Season the pot with pepper and ma' kamakh, oil and some spices, some sugar, wine vinegar, and five almonds ground up fine; add to the pot. Then break eggs over (the contents) and allow to settle. God willing.